UNLIGHTENMENT

A GUIDE TO HIGHER CONSCIOUSNESS FOR EVERYDAY PEOPLE

By Cathy Thorne

Adams Media

New York   London   Toronto   Sydney   New Delhi

Adams Media
An Imprint of Simon & Schuster, Inc.
57 Littlefield Street
Avon, Massachusetts 02322

First Adams Media hardcover edition NOVEMBER 2017

ADAMS MEDIA and colophon are trademarks of Simon and Schuster.

For information about special discounts for bulk purchases, please contact Simon & Schuster Special Sales at 1-866-506-1949 or business@simonandschuster.com.

The Simon & Schuster Speakers Bureau can bring authors to your live event. For more information or to book an event contact the Simon & Schuster Speakers Bureau at 1-866-248-3049 or visit our website at www.simonspeakers.com.

Interior design by Colleen Cunningham
Illustrations by Cathy Thorne

Manufactured in the United States of America

10 9 8 7 6 5 4 3 2 1

ISBN 978-1-5072-0507-5
ISBN 978-1-5072-0508-2 (ebook)

INTRODUCTION

enlightenment
a state of serenity achieved through
mindfulness, yoga, and meditation

unlightenment
when cookies work faster

We're all searching for that delightful, mysterious state of mind called enlightenment. Unfortunately, it's not as easy as those #LiveInTheMoment posts make it seem. It requires us to be perpetually aware, constantly present, and eternally mindful...but who has time for that?

Unlightenment gives you permission to take a step back and accept that serenity isn't that simple. These comics illustrate the search for higher meaning as it competes with the reality of hungry stomachs, ringing cell phones, and overactive minds.

If you can relate, *congratulations*! You're already on your way through *un*lightenment.

—

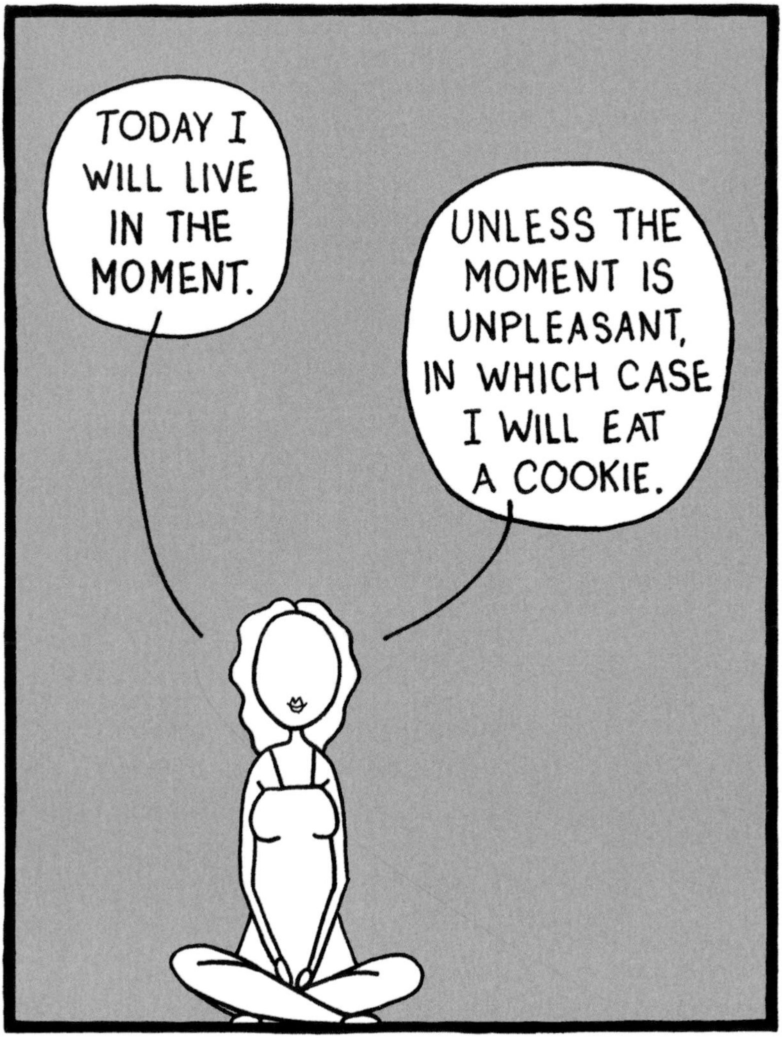
TODAY I WILL LIVE IN THE MOMENT.
UNLESS THE MOMENT IS UNPLEASANT, IN WHICH CASE I WILL EAT A COOKIE.

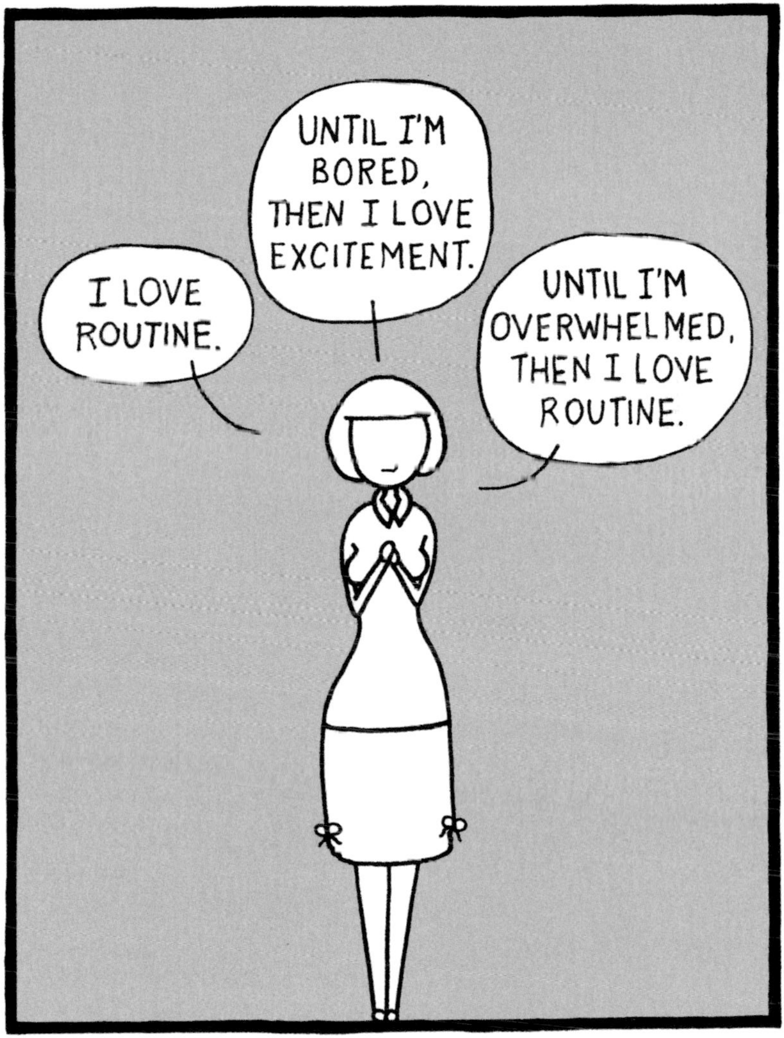
I LOVE ROUTINE.
UNTIL I'M BORED, THEN I LOVE EXCITEMENT.
UNTIL I'M OVERWHELMED, THEN I LOVE ROUTINE.

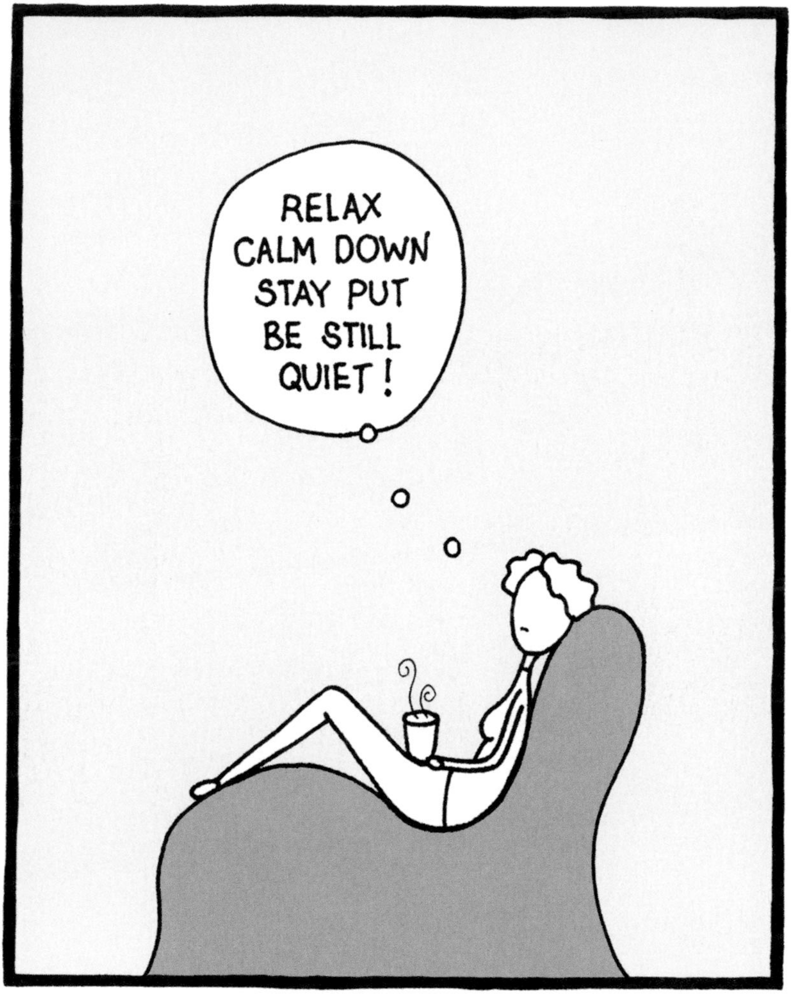
RELAX
CALM DOWN
STAY PUT
BE STILL
QUIET!

TAKING IT EASY IS HARD.

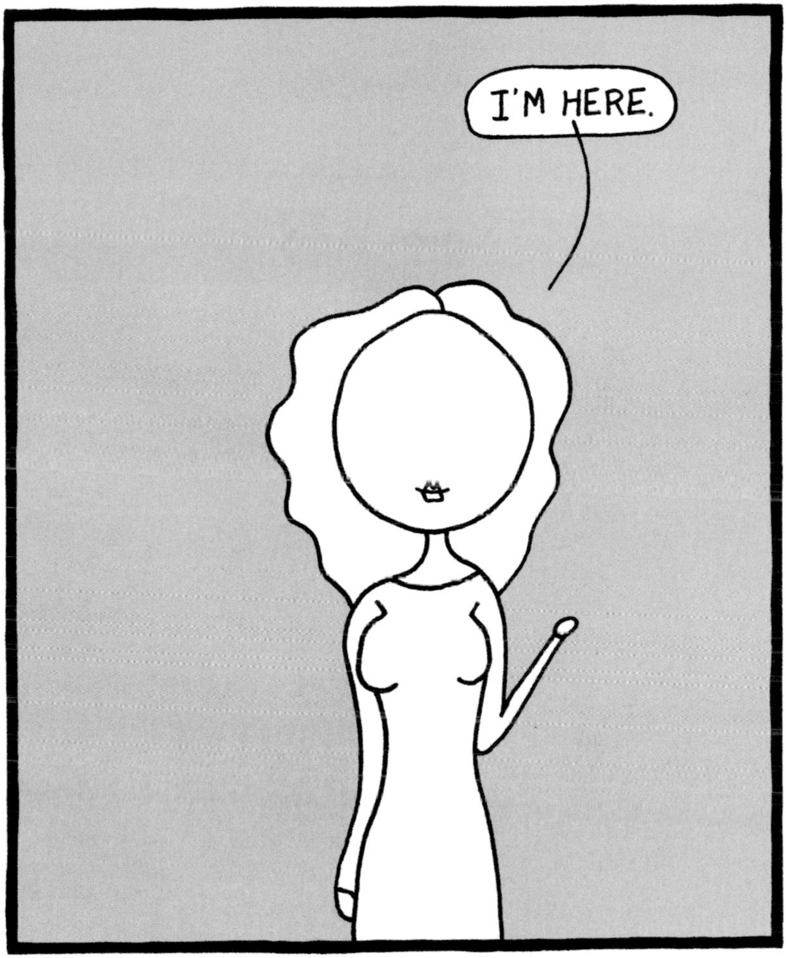
I'M HERE.
THE SECRET TO A SUCCESSFUL
LIFE IS SHOWING UP.

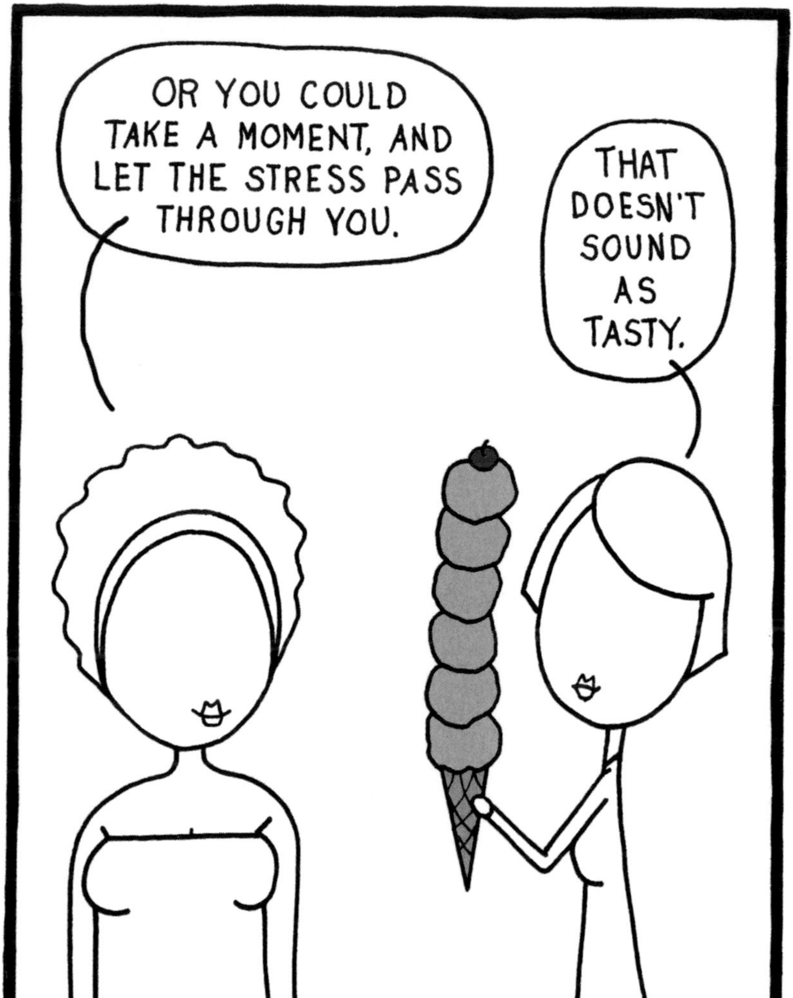
OR YOU COULD TAKE A MOMENT, AND LET THE STRESS PASS THROUGH YOU.
THAT DOESN'T SOUND AS TASTY.

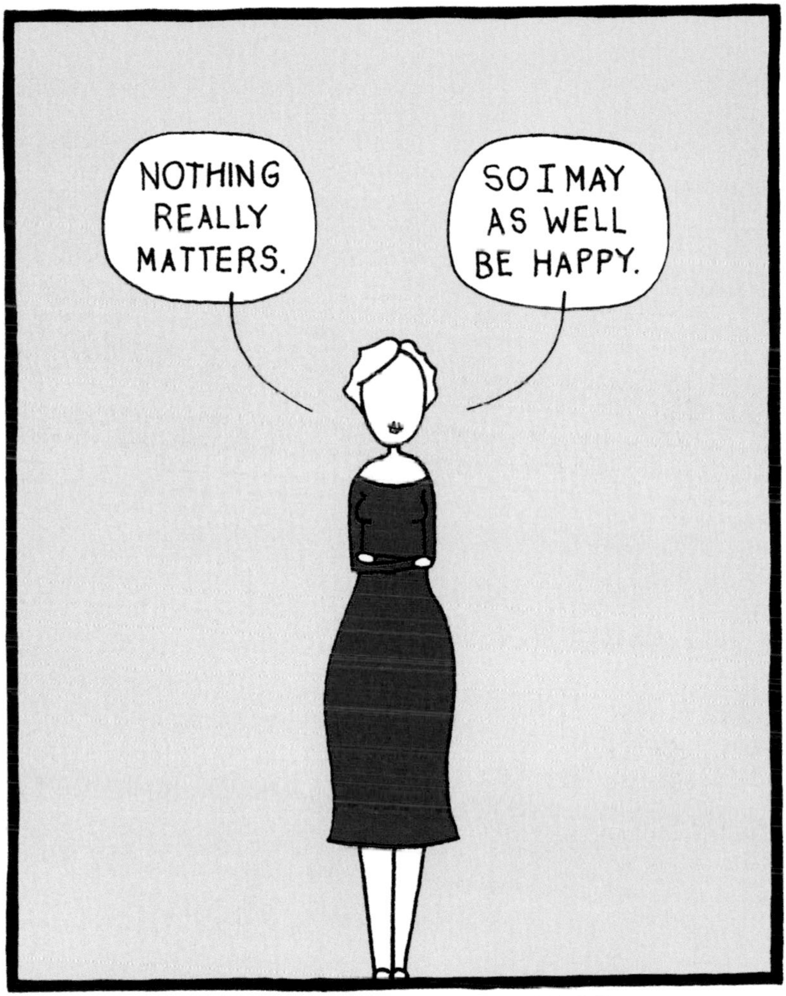
NOTHING REALLY MATTERS.
SO I MAY AS WELL BE HAPPY.

THE OPTIMISTIC PESSIMIST.

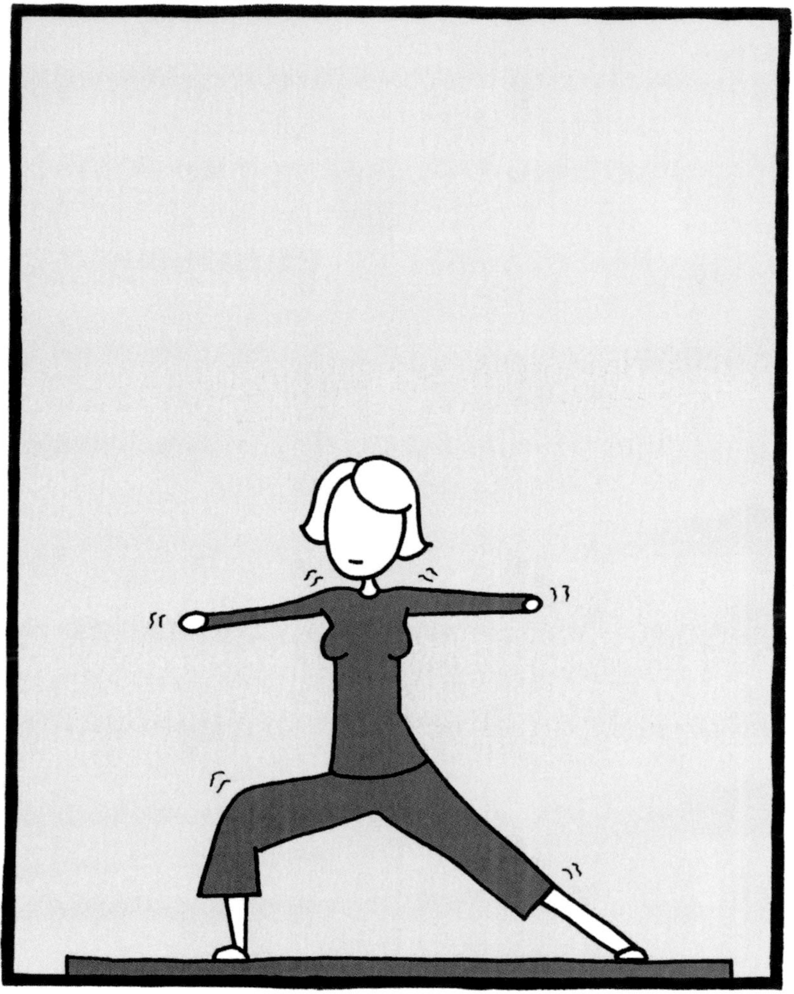

WARRIOR QUIVER POSE

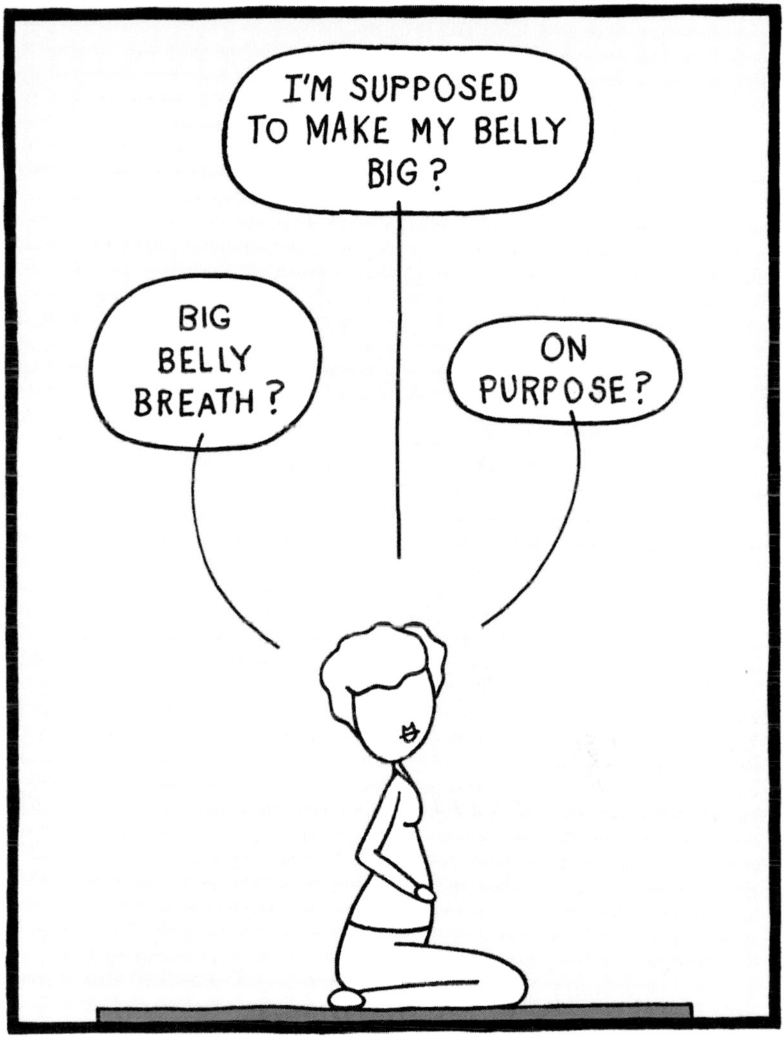
BIG BELLY BREATH?
I'M SUPPOSED TO MAKE MY BELLY BIG?
ON PURPOSE?

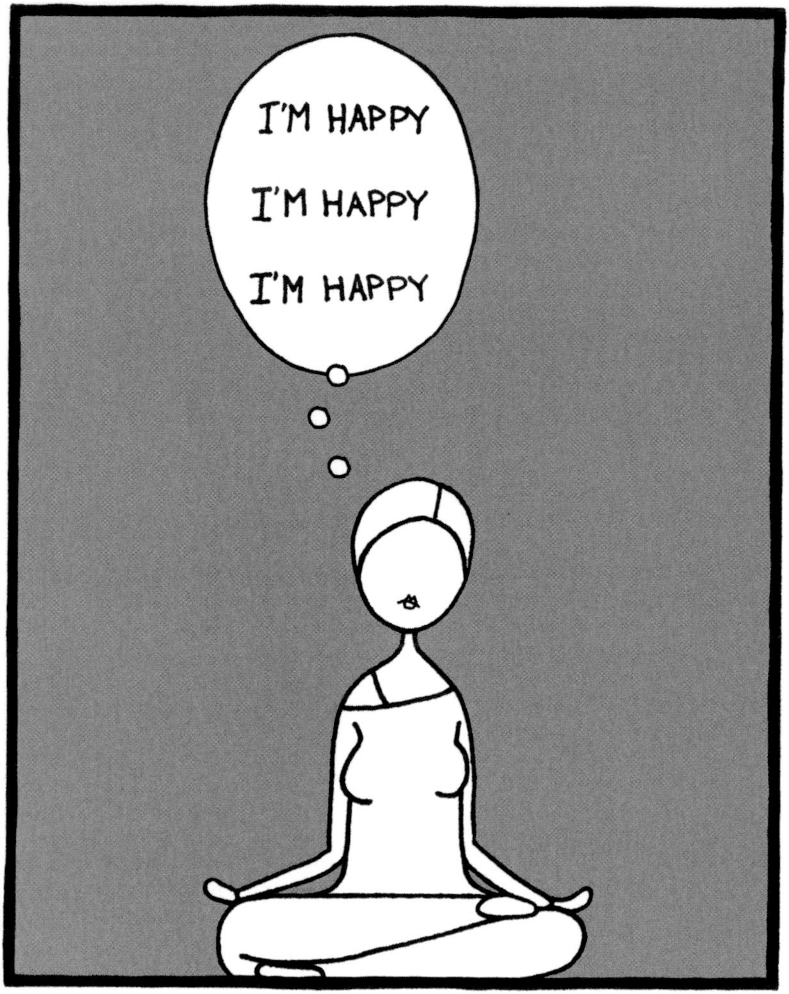
I'M HAPPY
I'M HAPPY
I'M HAPPY

HAPPINESS HARASSMENT.

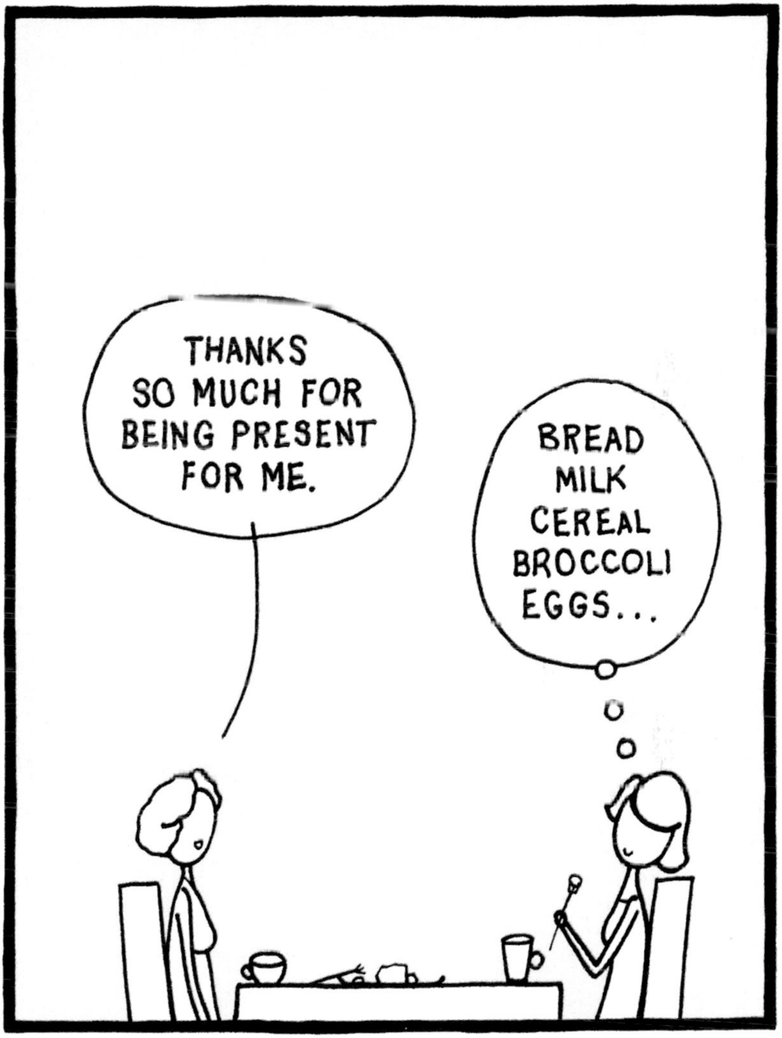
THANKS SO MUCH FOR BEING PRESENT FOR ME.
BREAD MILK CEREAL BROCCOLI EGGS...

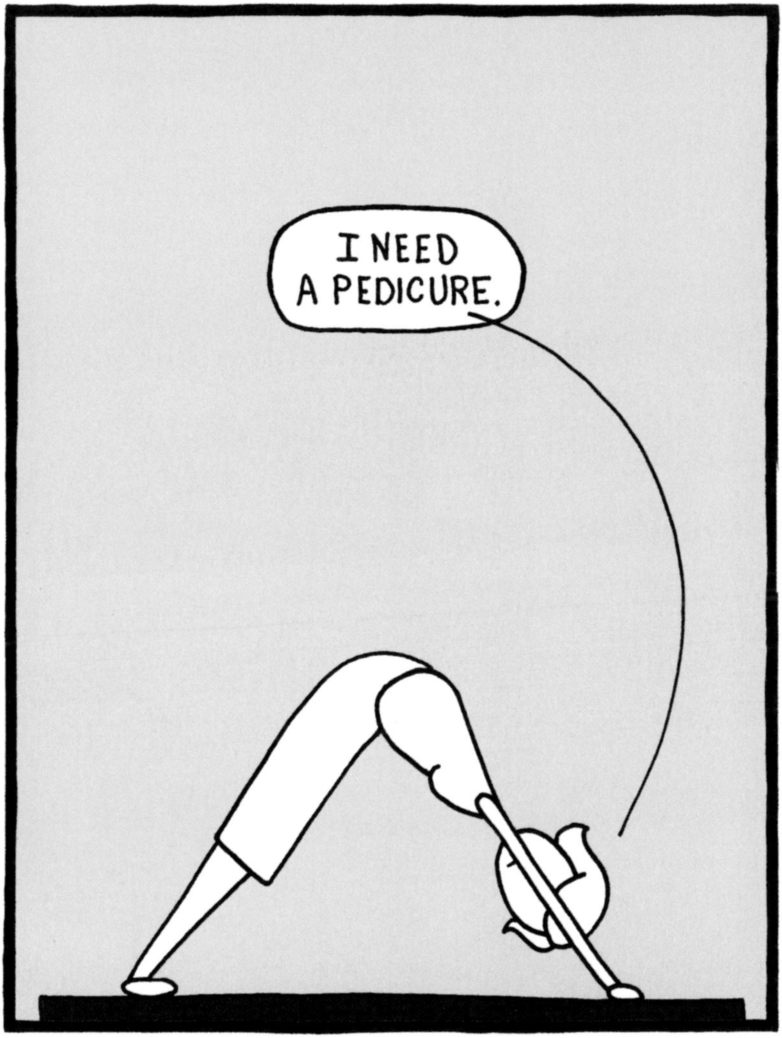
I NEED A PEDICURE.

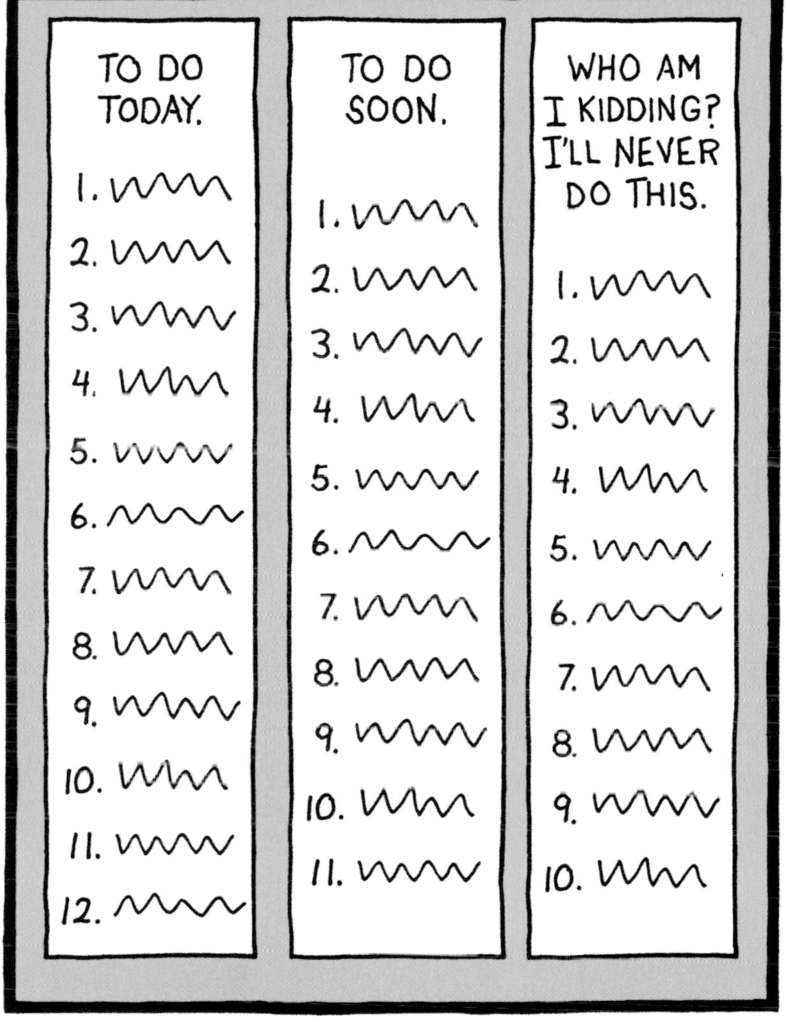
TO DO TODAY.
1. 2. 3. 4. 5. 6. 7. 8. 9. 10. 11. 12.
TO DO SOON.
1. 2. 3. 4. 5. 6. 7. 8. 9. 10. 11.
WHO AM I KIDDING? I'LL NEVER DO THIS.
1. 2. 3. 4. 5. 6. 7. 8. 9. 10.

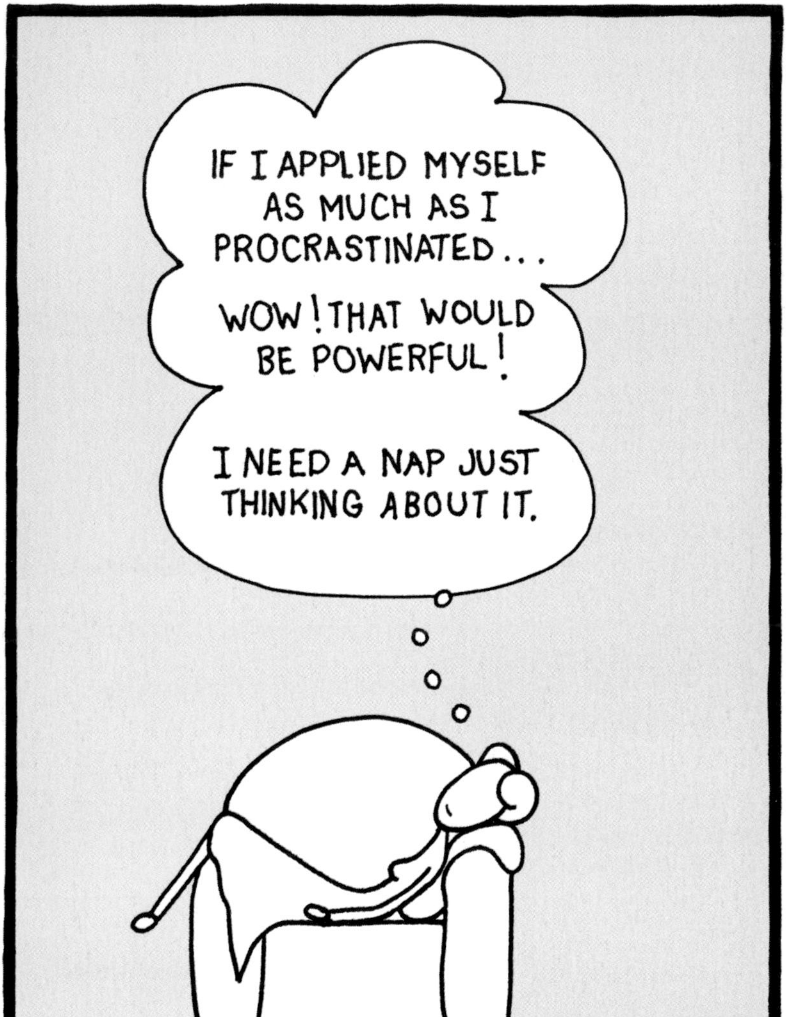
IF I APPLIED MYSELF AS MUCH AS I PROCRASTINATED . . .
WOW! THAT WOULD BE POWERFUL!
I NEED A NAP JUST THINKING ABOUT IT.

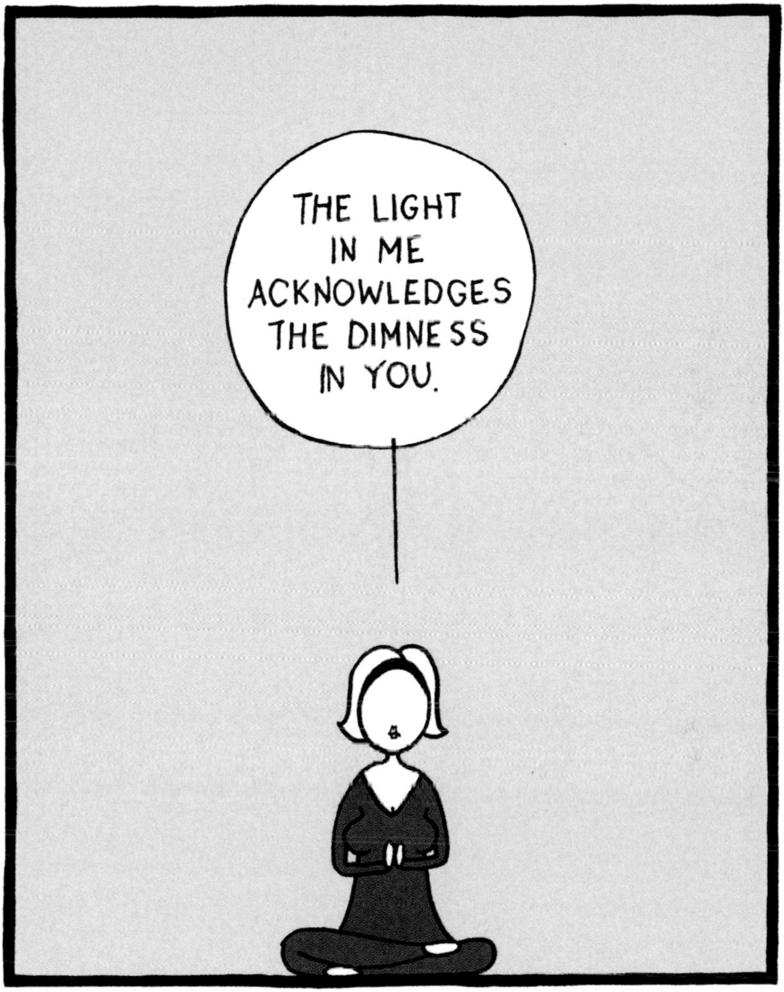
THE LIGHT IN ME ACKNOWLEDGES THE DIMNESS IN YOU.

UNLIGHTENMENT

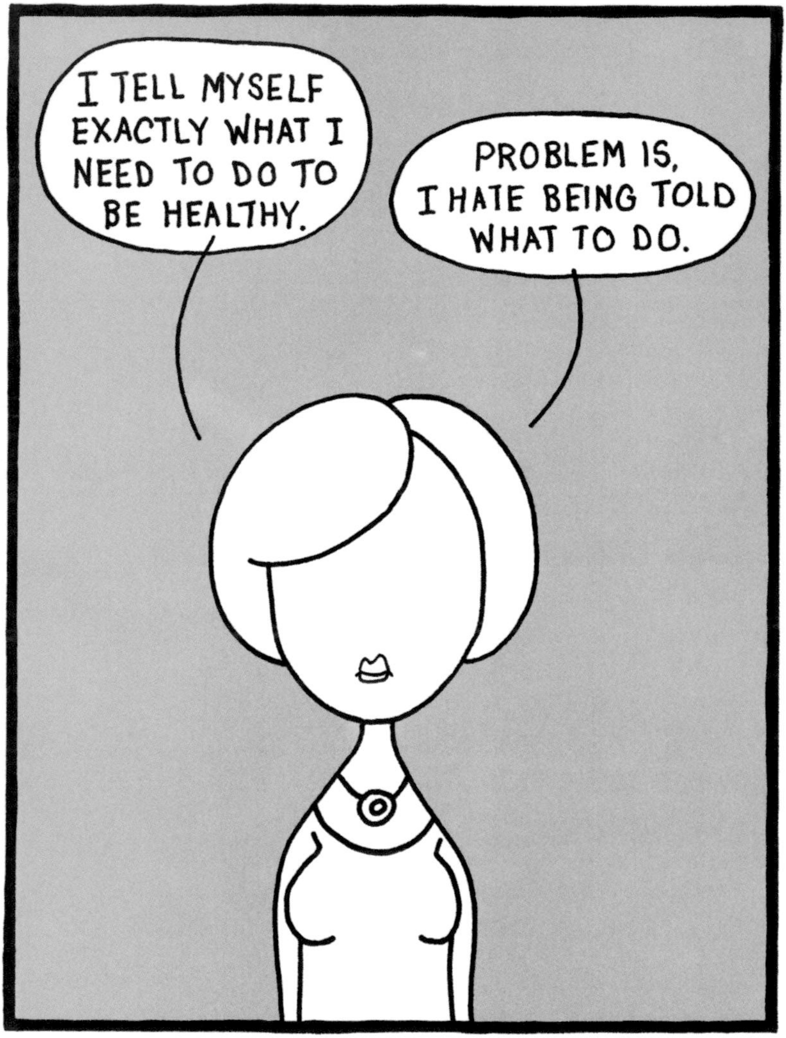
I TELL MYSELF EXACTLY WHAT I NEED TO DO TO BE HEALTHY.
PROBLEM IS, I HATE BEING TOLD WHAT TO DO.

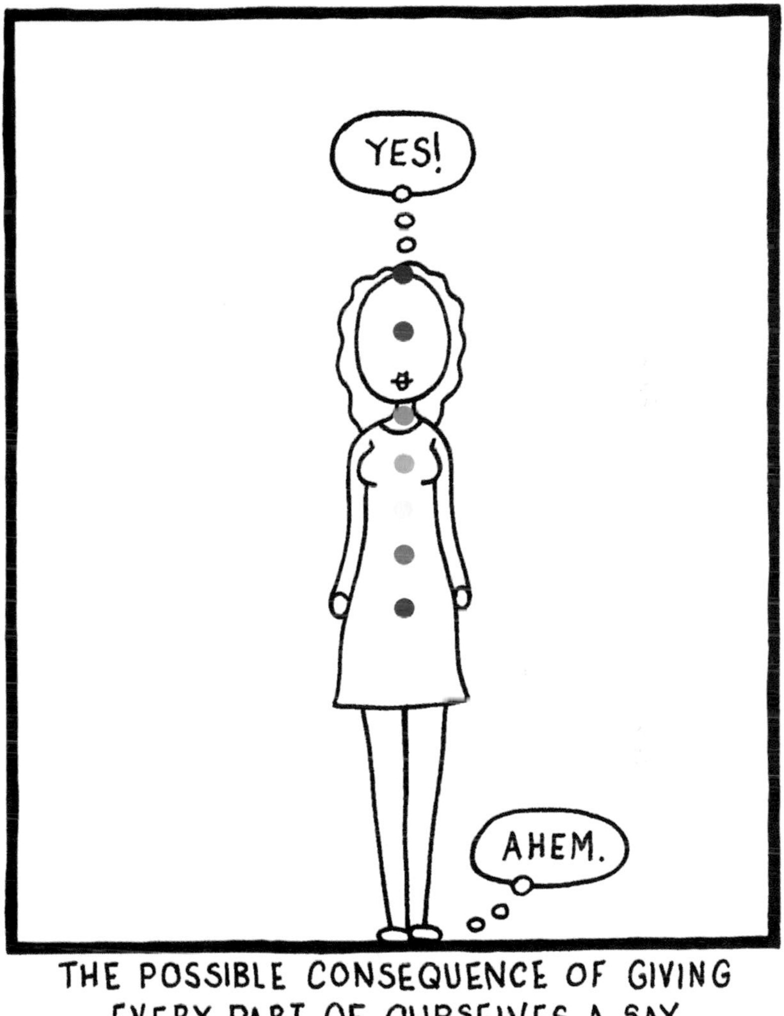
YES!
AHEM.

THE POSSIBLE CONSEQUENCE OF GIVING EVERY PART OF OURSELVES A SAY.

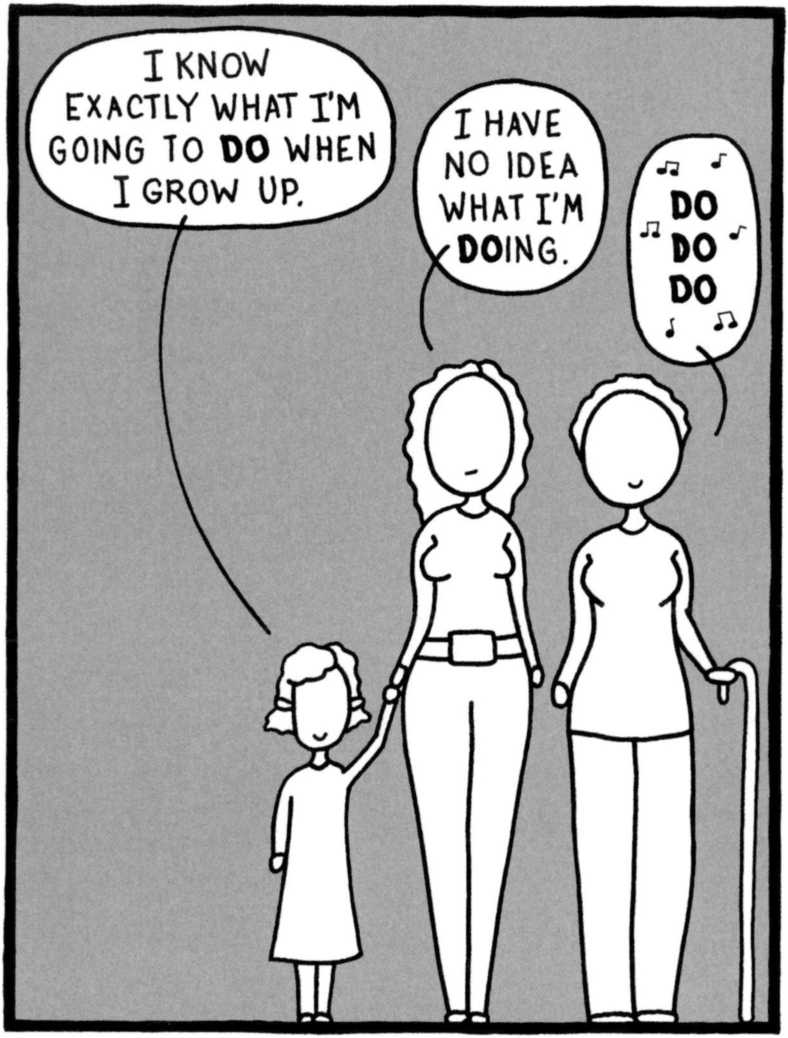
I KNOW EXACTLY WHAT I'M GOING TO **DO** WHEN I GROW UP.
I HAVE NO IDEA WHAT I'M **DO**ING.
DO DO DO

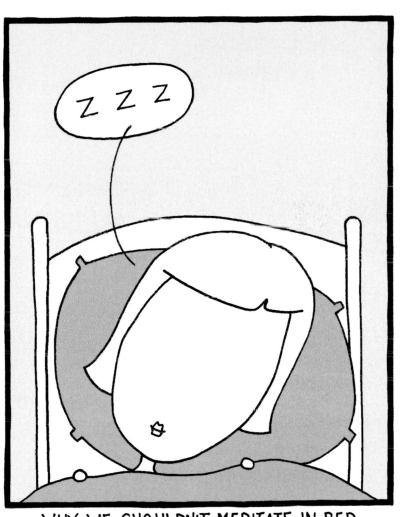

WHY WE SHOULDN'T MEDITATE IN BED.

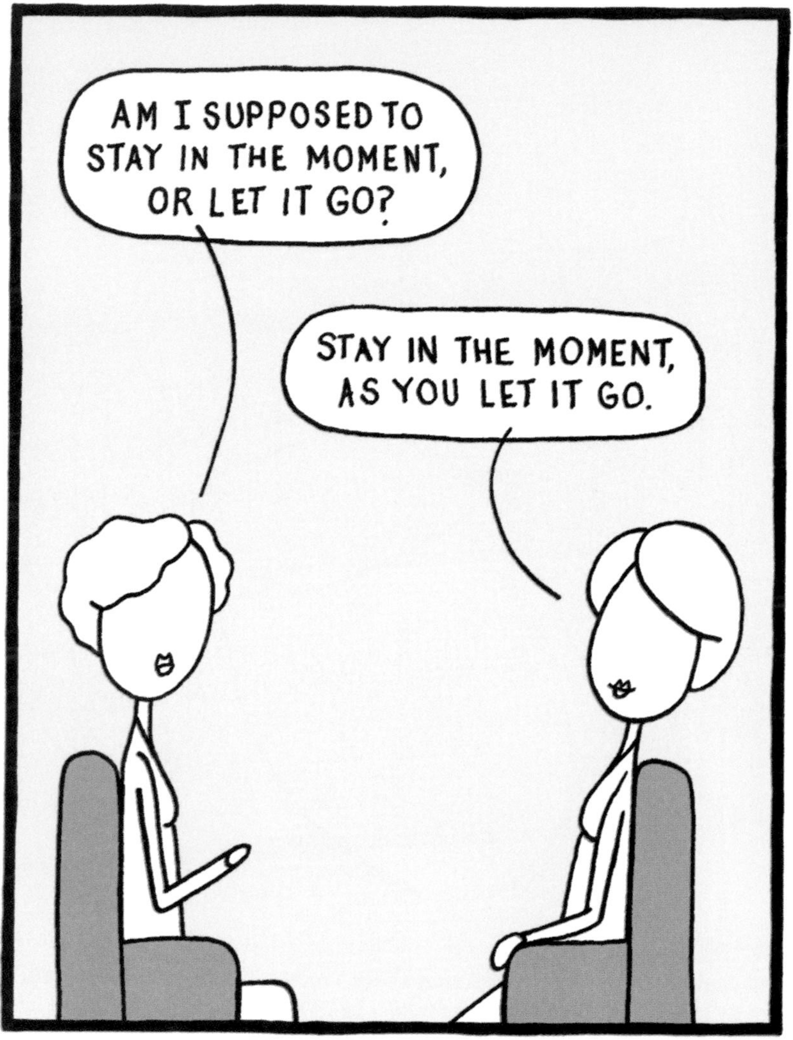
AM I SUPPOSED TO STAY IN THE MOMENT, OR LET IT GO?
STAY IN THE MOMENT, AS YOU LET IT GO.

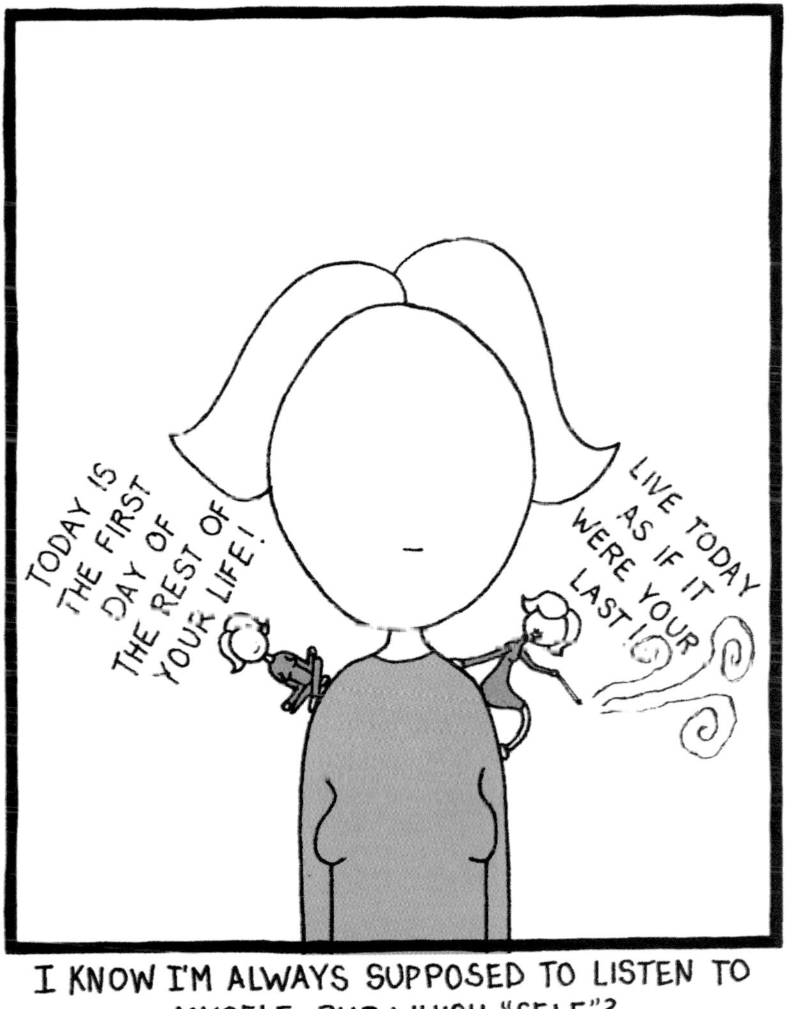
TODAY IS THE FIRST DAY OF THE REST OF YOUR LIFE!
LIVE TODAY AS IF IT WERE YOUR LAST!

I KNOW I'M ALWAYS SUPPOSED TO LISTEN TO MYSELF, BUT WHICH "SELF"?

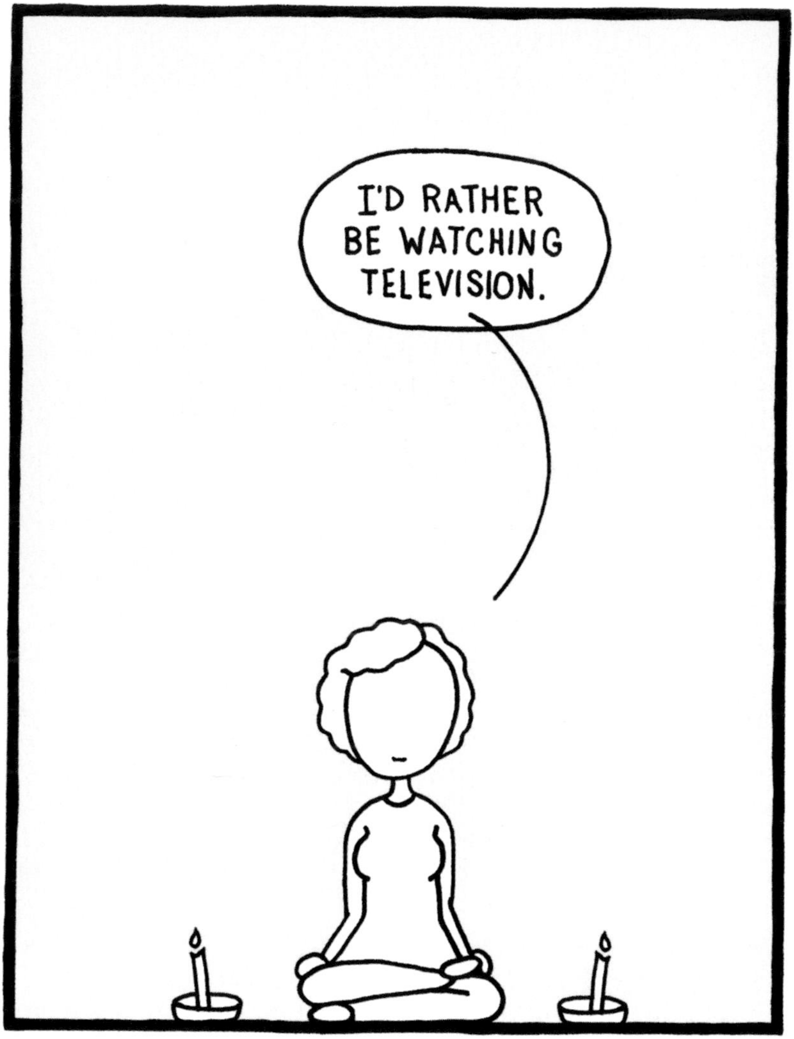
I'D RATHER BE WATCHING TELEVISION.

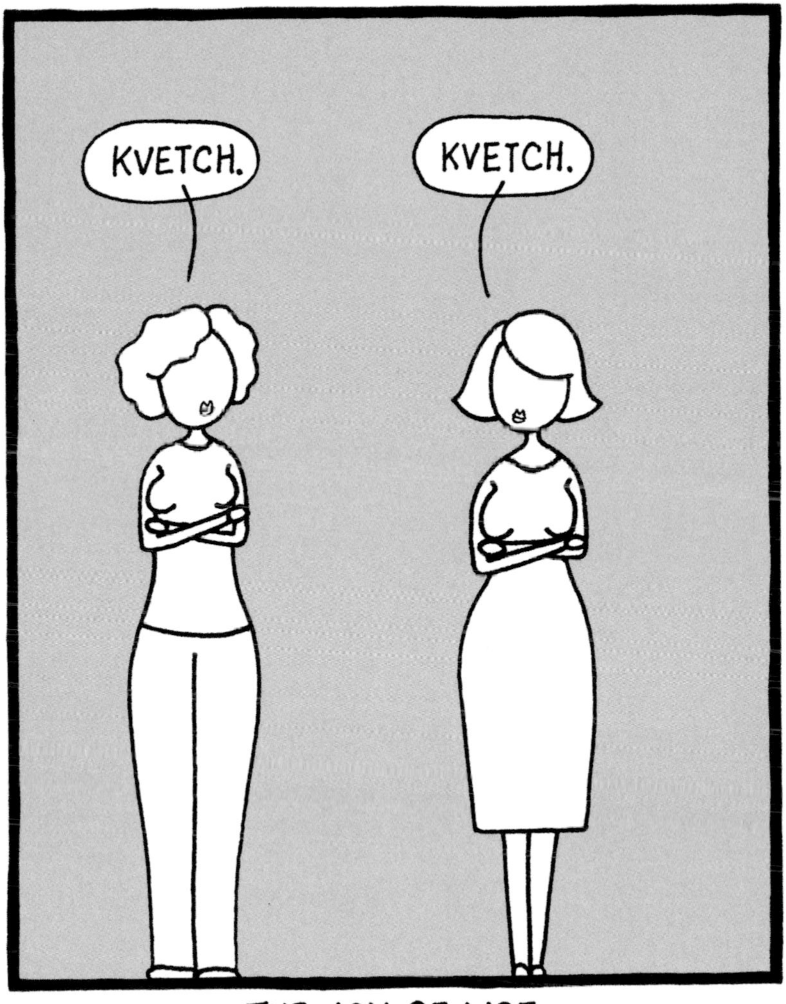
KVETCH.
KVETCH.

THE JOY OF WOE.

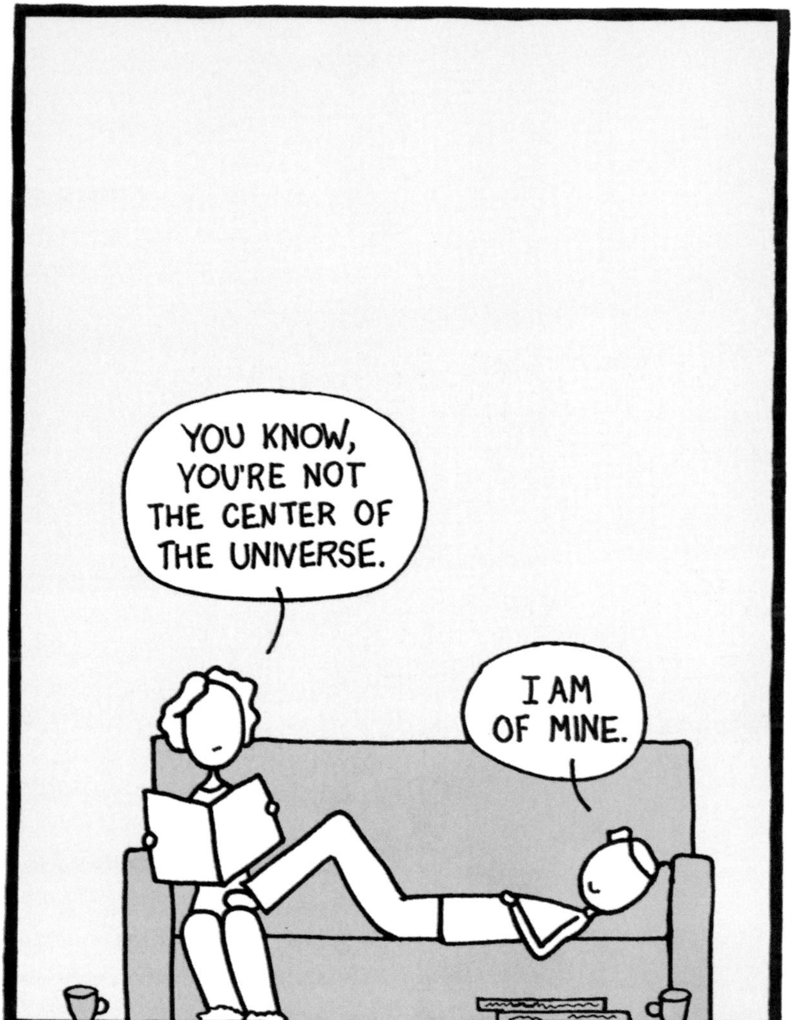
YOU KNOW, YOU'RE NOT THE CENTER OF THE UNIVERSE.
I AM OF MINE.

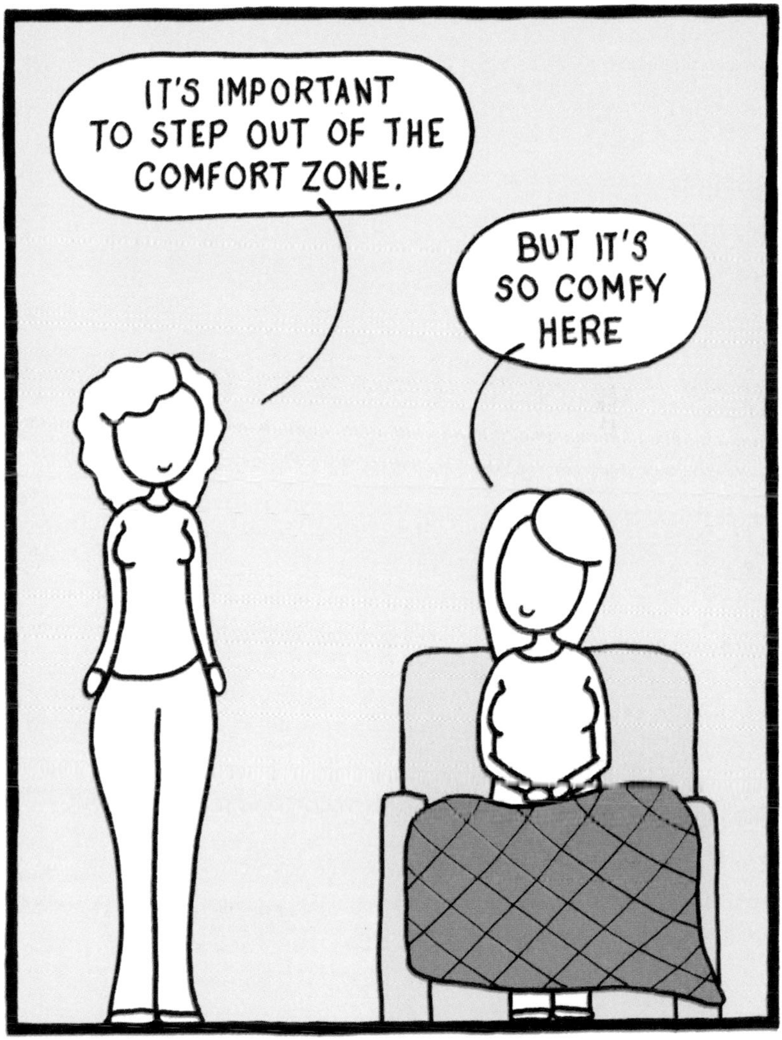
IT'S IMPORTANT TO STEP OUT OF THE COMFORT ZONE.
BUT IT'S SO COMFY HERE

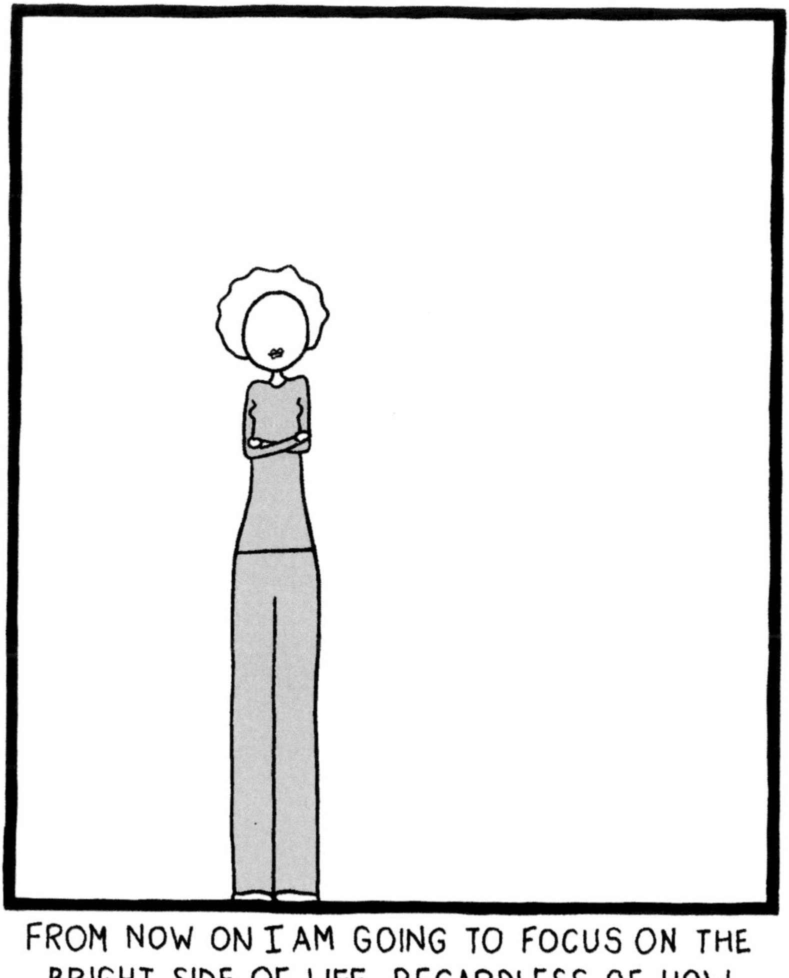

FROM NOW ON I AM GOING TO FOCUS ON THE BRIGHT SIDE OF LIFE, REGARDLESS OF HOW MISERABLE IT MAKES ME.

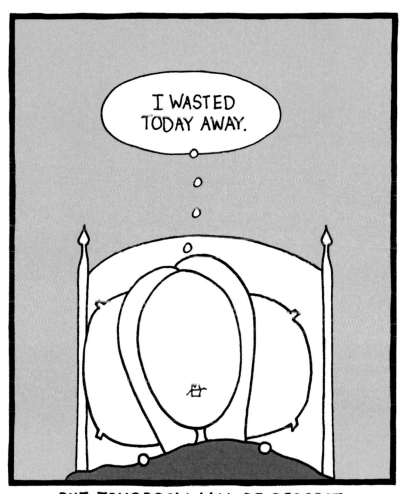

BUT TOMORROW WILL BE PERFECT,
OR AT LEAST THAT'S MY INTENTION.

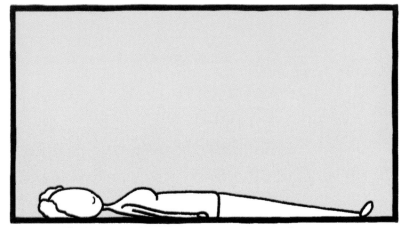

THE BEST PART OF YOGA CLASS.

THE WORST PART OF YOGA CLASS.

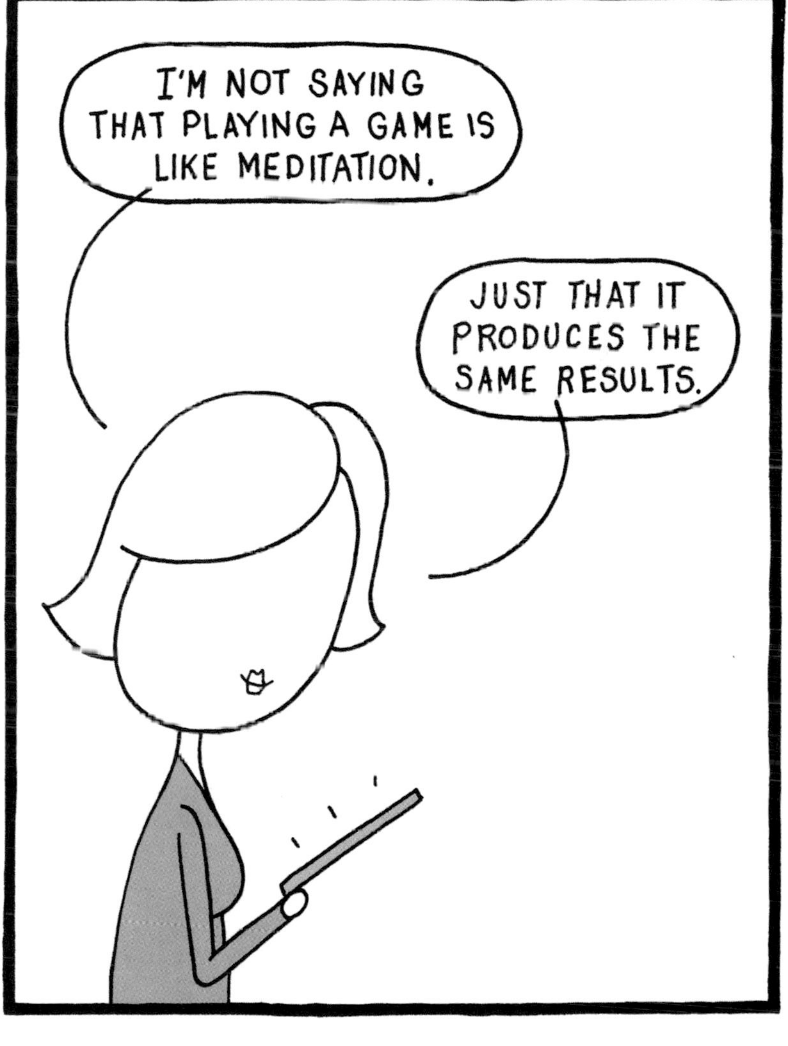
I'M NOT SAYING THAT PLAYING A GAME IS LIKE MEDITATION.
JUST THAT IT PRODUCES THE SAME RESULTS.

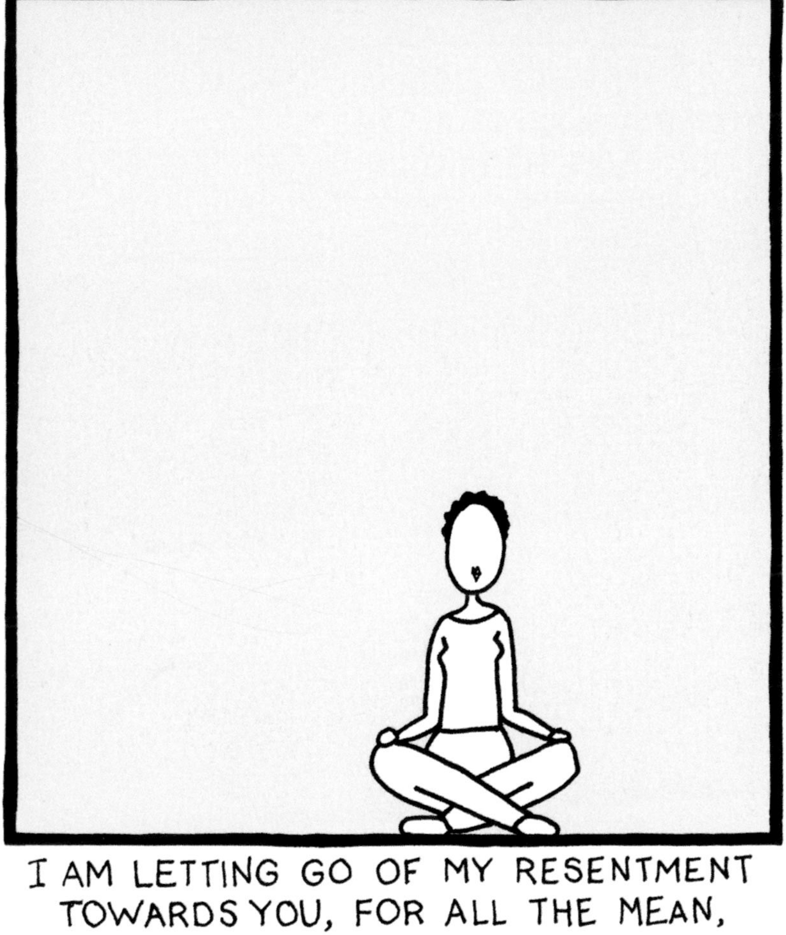

I AM LETTING GO OF MY RESENTMENT TOWARDS YOU, FOR ALL THE MEAN, NASTY, AND UNFORGIVABLE THINGS YOU HAVE DONE TO ME. YOU LOUSY BUM.

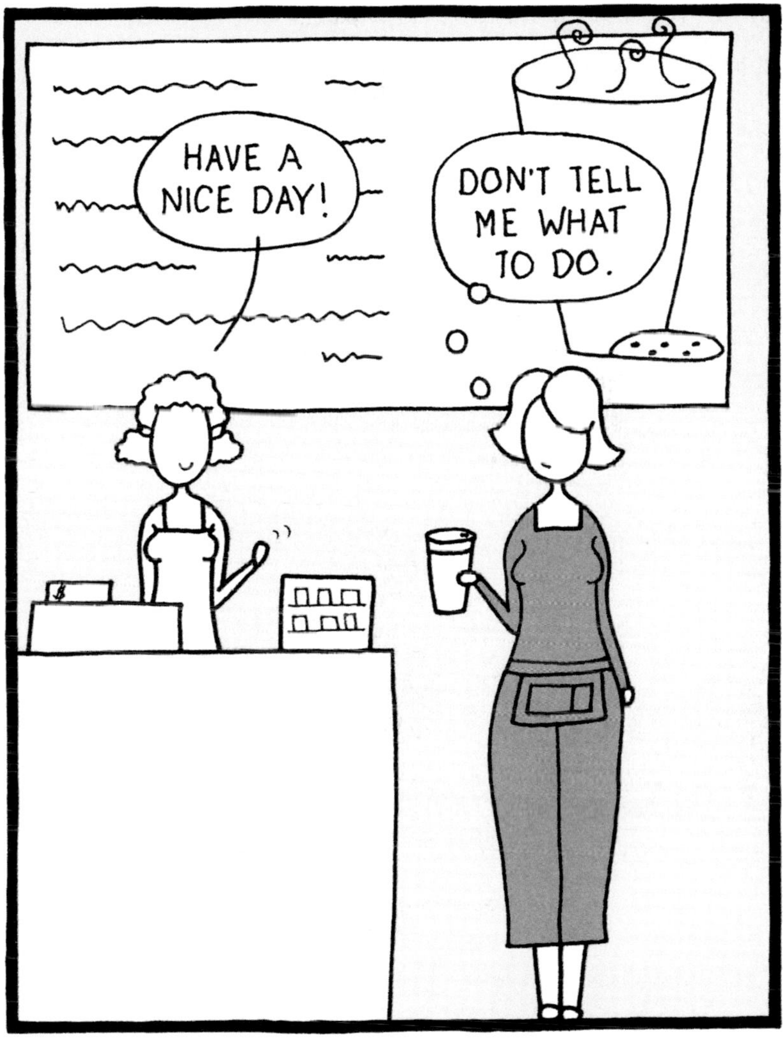
HAVE A NICE DAY!
DON'T TELL ME WHAT TO DO.

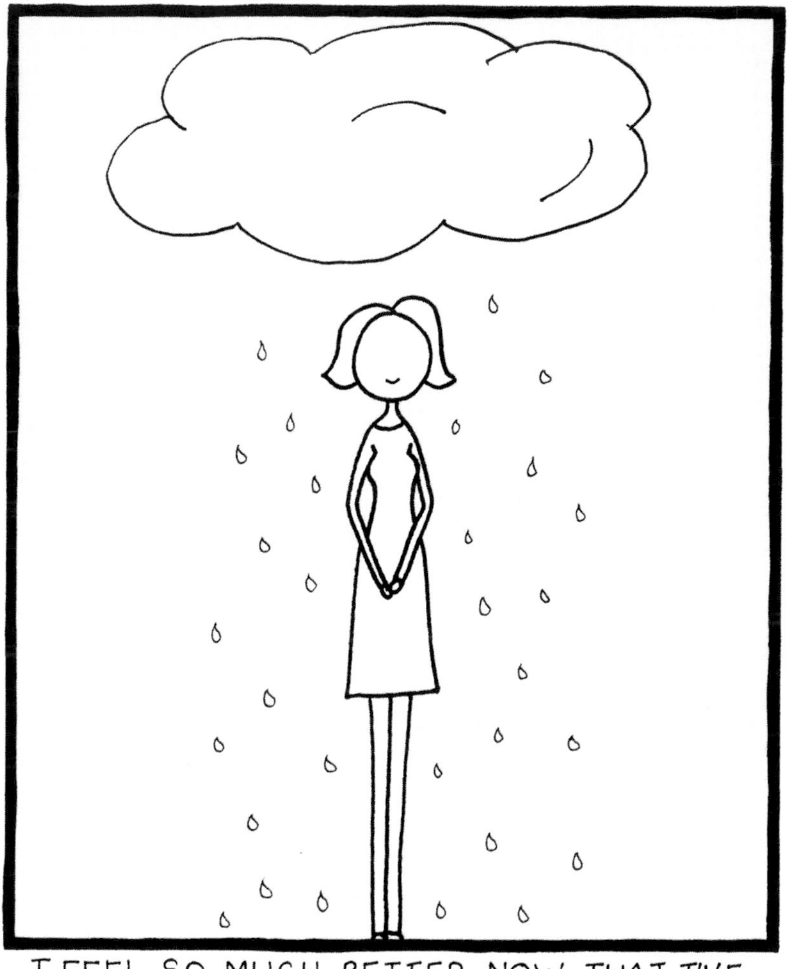

I FEEL SO MUCH BETTER NOW THAT I'VE ACCEPTED HOW AWFUL I FEEL.

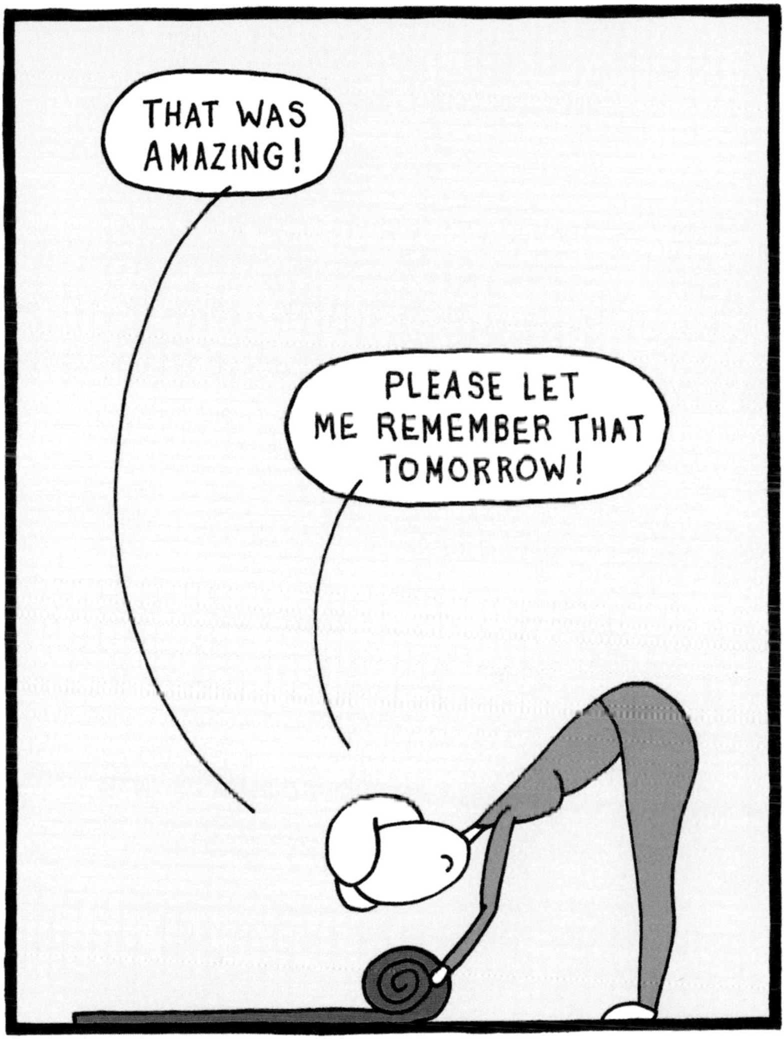
THAT WAS AMAZING!
PLEASE LET ME REMEMBER THAT TOMORROW!

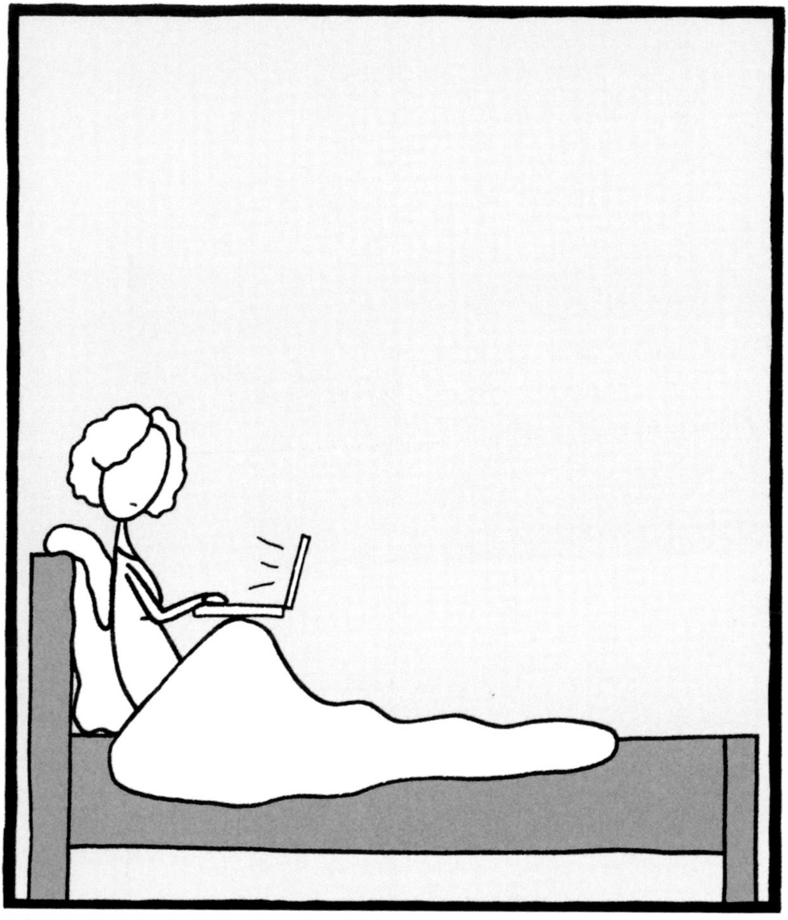

YOU KNOW IT'S TIME FOR AN ELECTRONIC CLEANSE WHEN YOU'RE CREEPING YOUR EX-BOYFRIEND'S WIFE'S COUSIN'S SISTER'S FRIEND'S WALL.

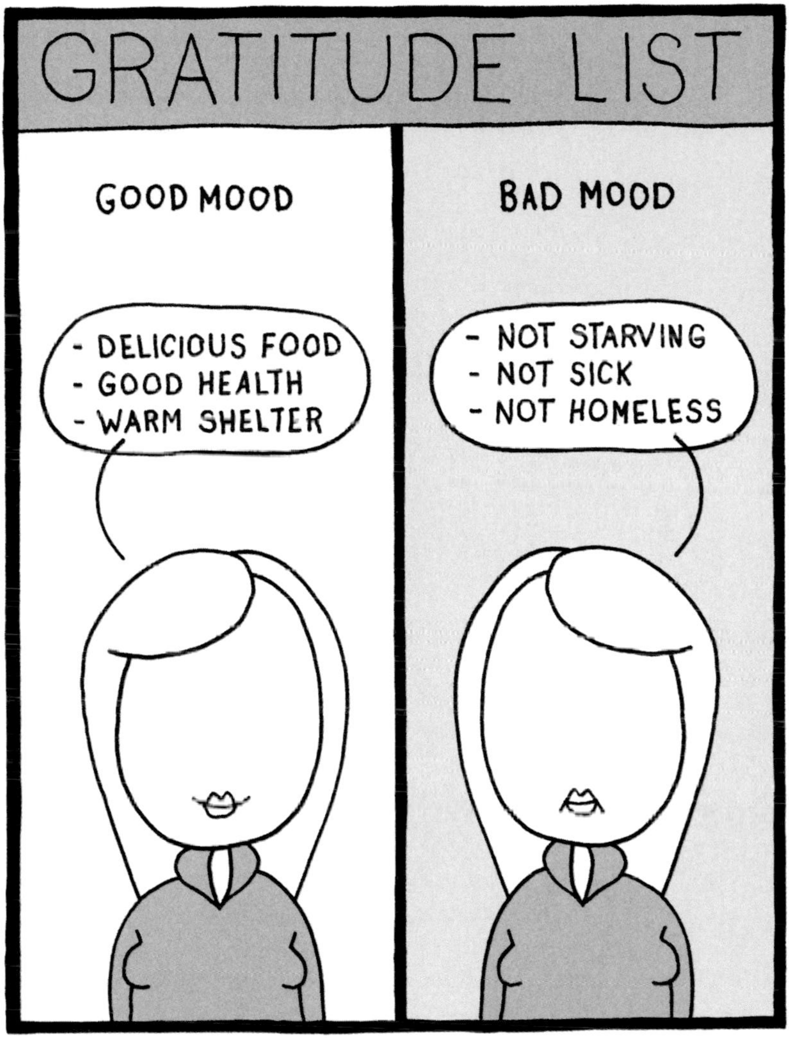
GRATITUDE LIST
GOOD MOOD
BAD MOOD
- DELICIOUS FOOD
- GOOD HEALTH
- WARM SHELTER
- NOT STARVING
- NOT SICK
- NOT HOMELESS

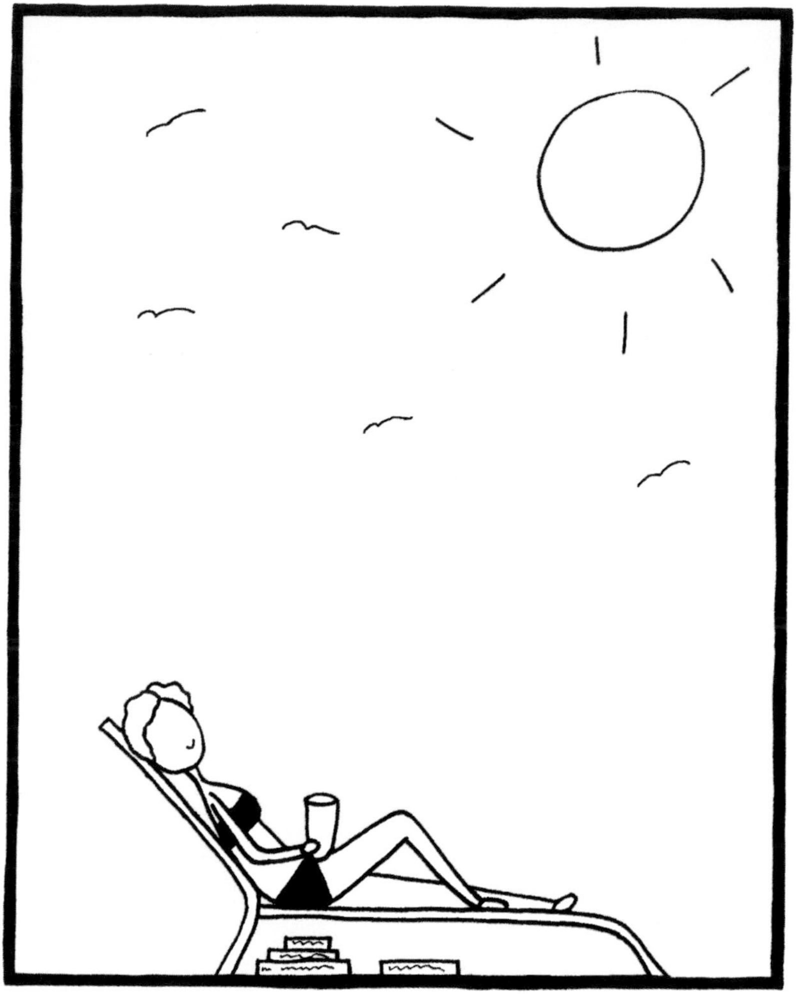

OUTER PEACE IS NICE TOO.

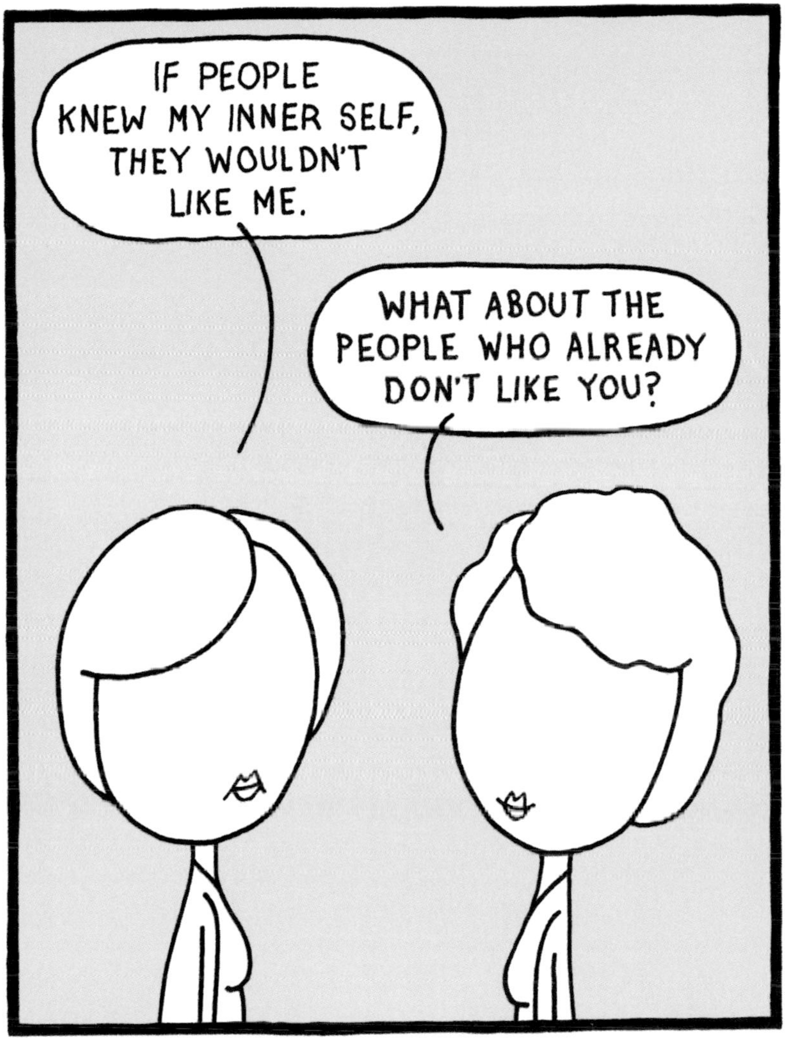
IF PEOPLE KNEW MY INNER SELF, THEY WOULDN'T LIKE ME.
WHAT ABOUT THE PEOPLE WHO ALREADY DON'T LIKE YOU?

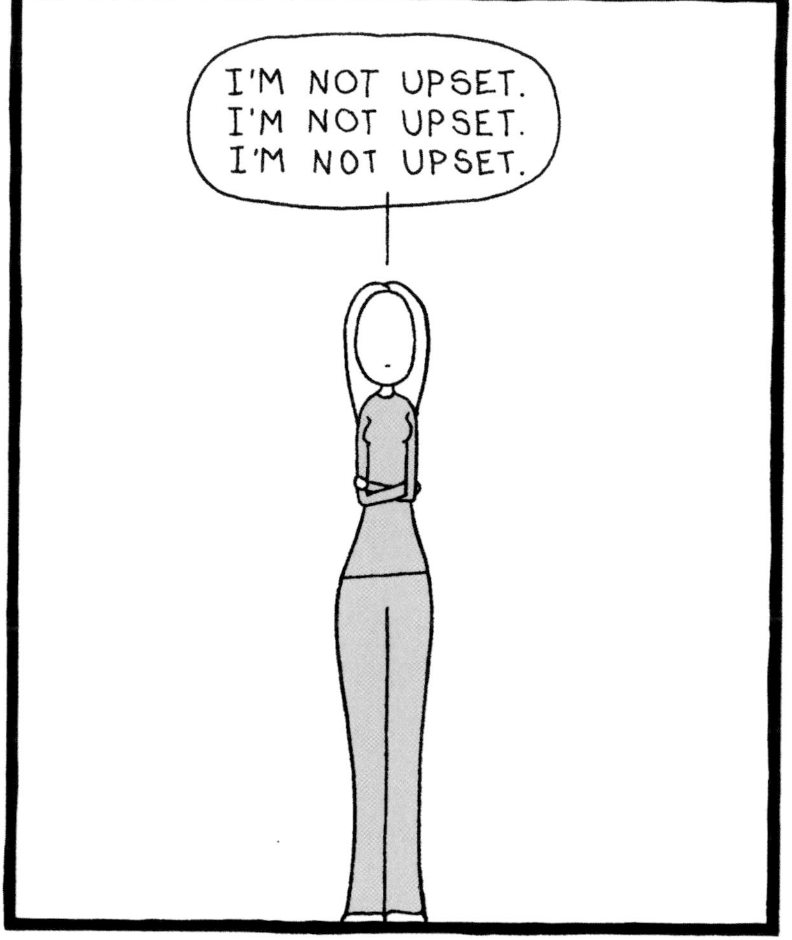
I'M NOT UPSET.
I'M NOT UPSET.
I'M NOT UPSET.

YOU CAN FIGHT A FEELING,
BUT YOU CAN'T WIN.

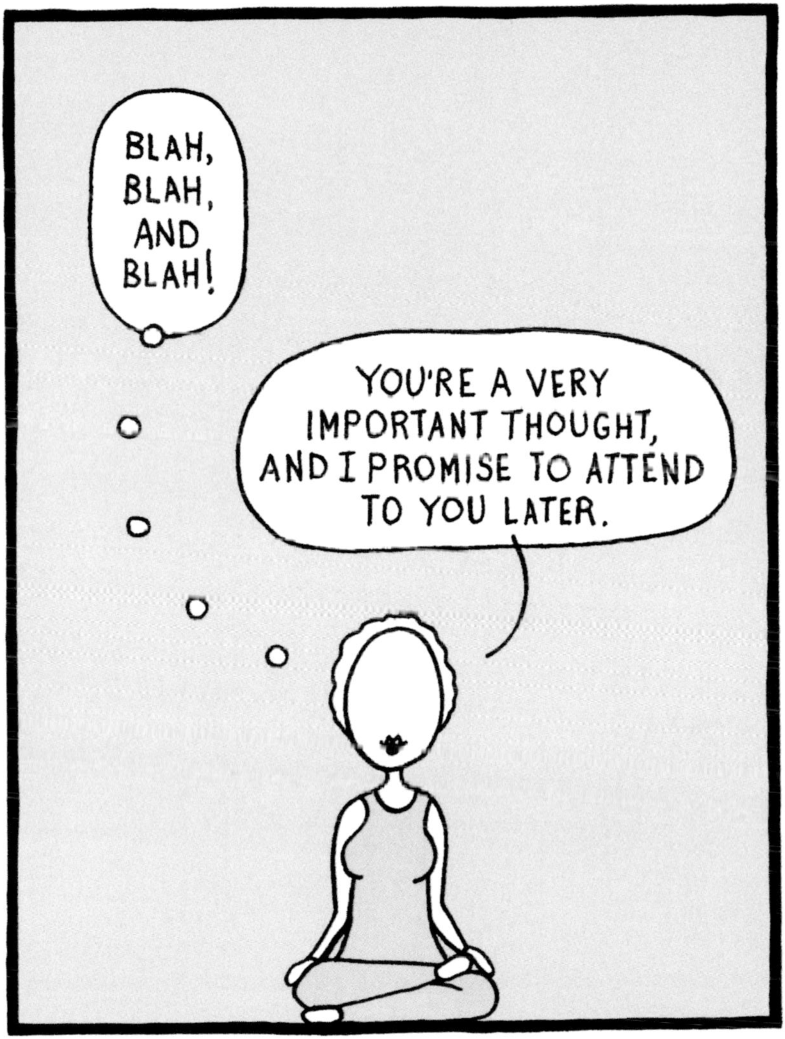
BLAH, BLAH, AND BLAH!
YOU'RE A VERY IMPORTANT THOUGHT, AND I PROMISE TO ATTEND TO YOU LATER.

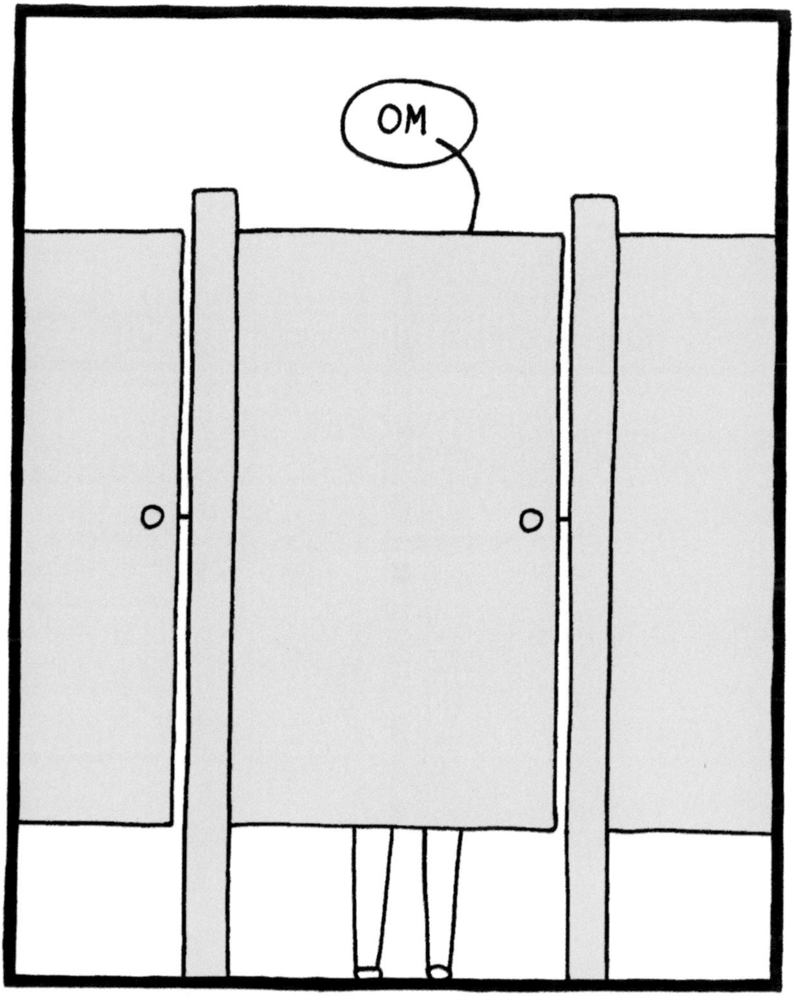
OM

MEDITATION-ON-THE-GO

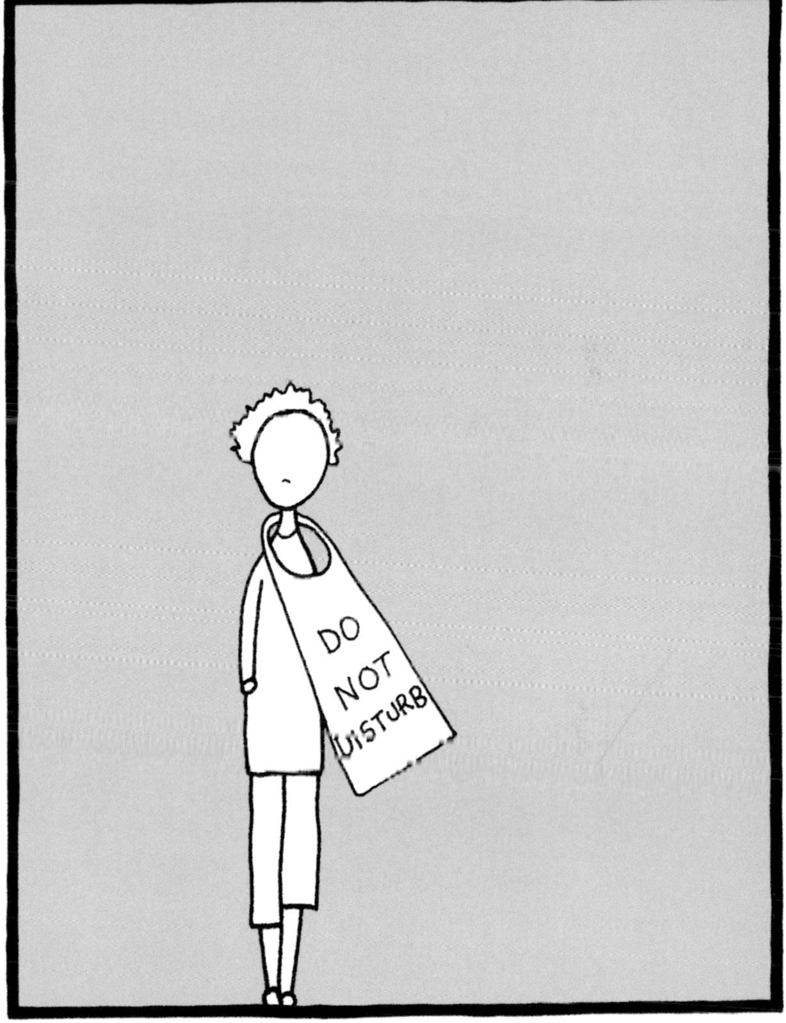
DO
NOT
DISTURB

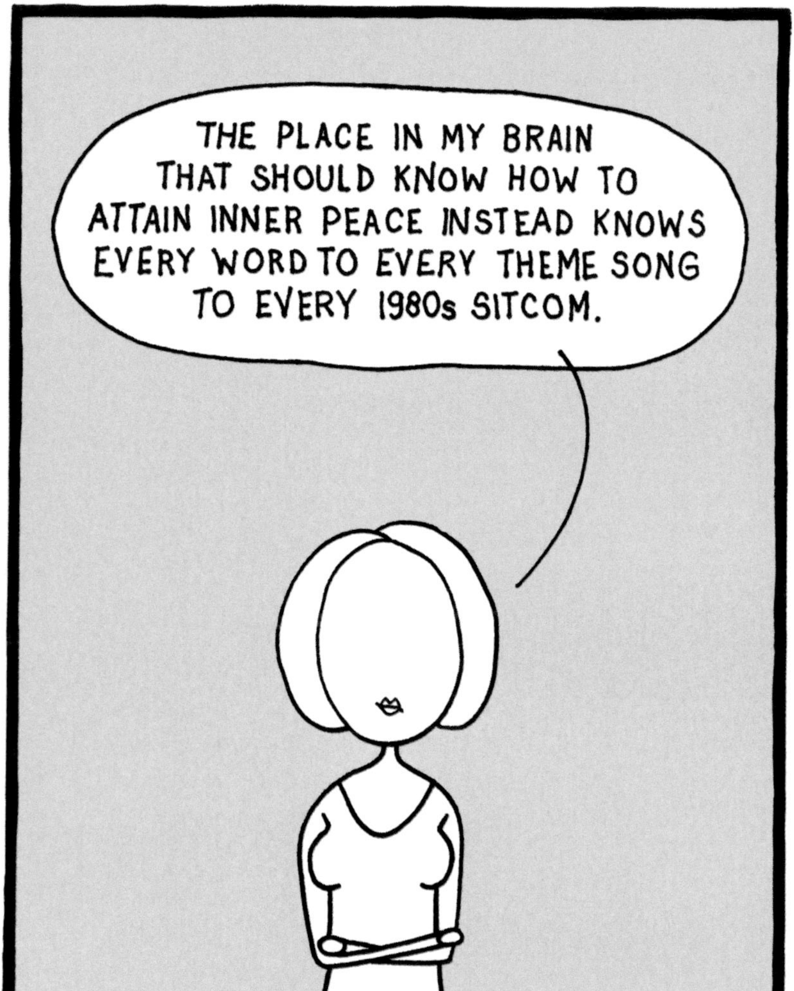
THE PLACE IN MY BRAIN THAT SHOULD KNOW HOW TO ATTAIN INNER PEACE INSTEAD KNOWS EVERY WORD TO EVERY THEME SONG TO EVERY 1980s SITCOM.

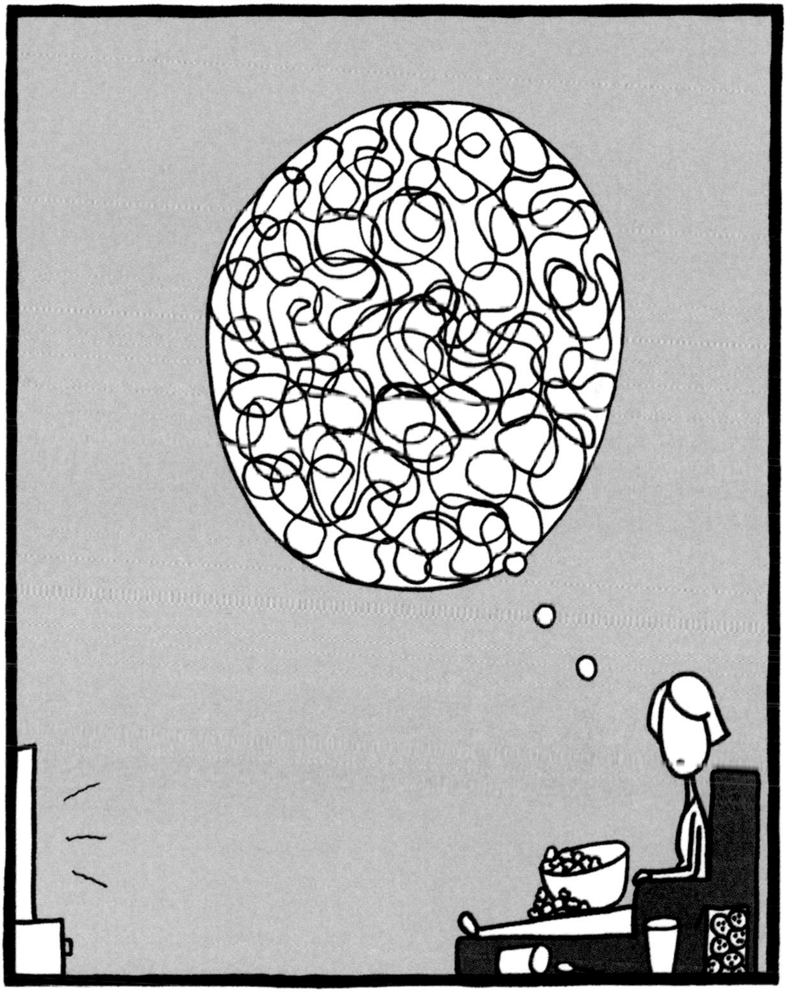

JUNK TV, JUNK FOOD, JUNK THOUGHTS.

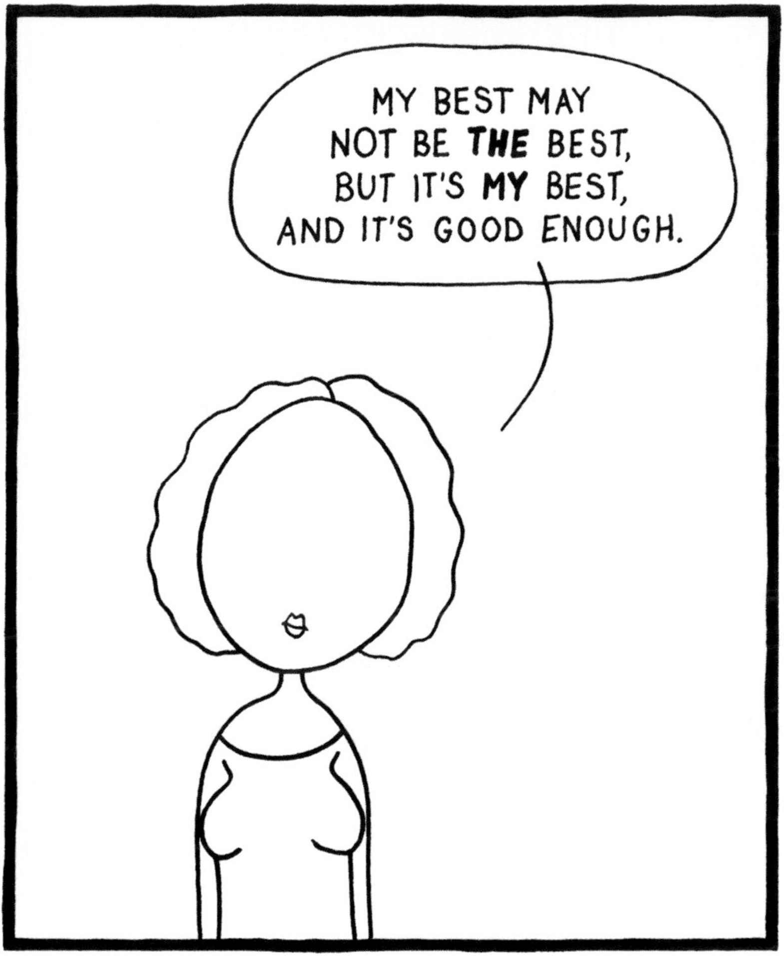
MY BEST MAY NOT BE **THE** BEST, BUT IT'S **MY** BEST, AND IT'S GOOD ENOUGH.

OR AT LEAST THAT'S WHAT I'M SUPPOSED TO TELL MYSELF.

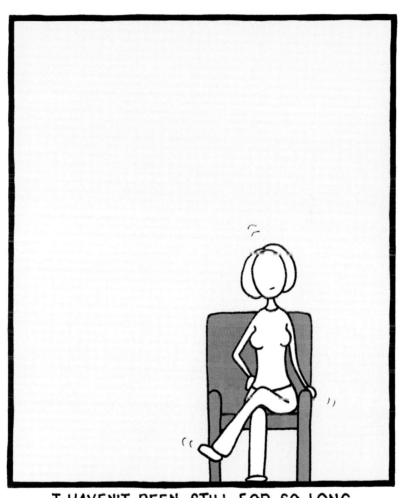

I HAVEN'T BEEN STILL FOR SO LONG,
I'M NOT SURE I STILL KNOW HOW TO BE.

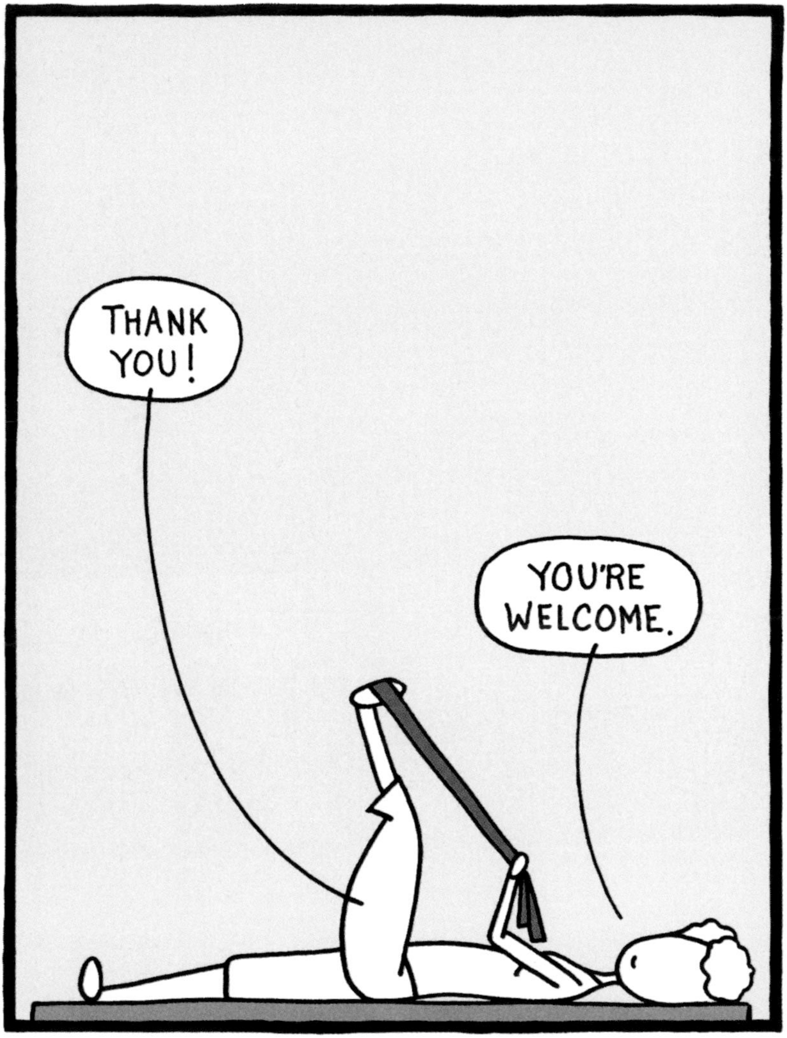
THANK YOU!
YOU'RE WELCOME.

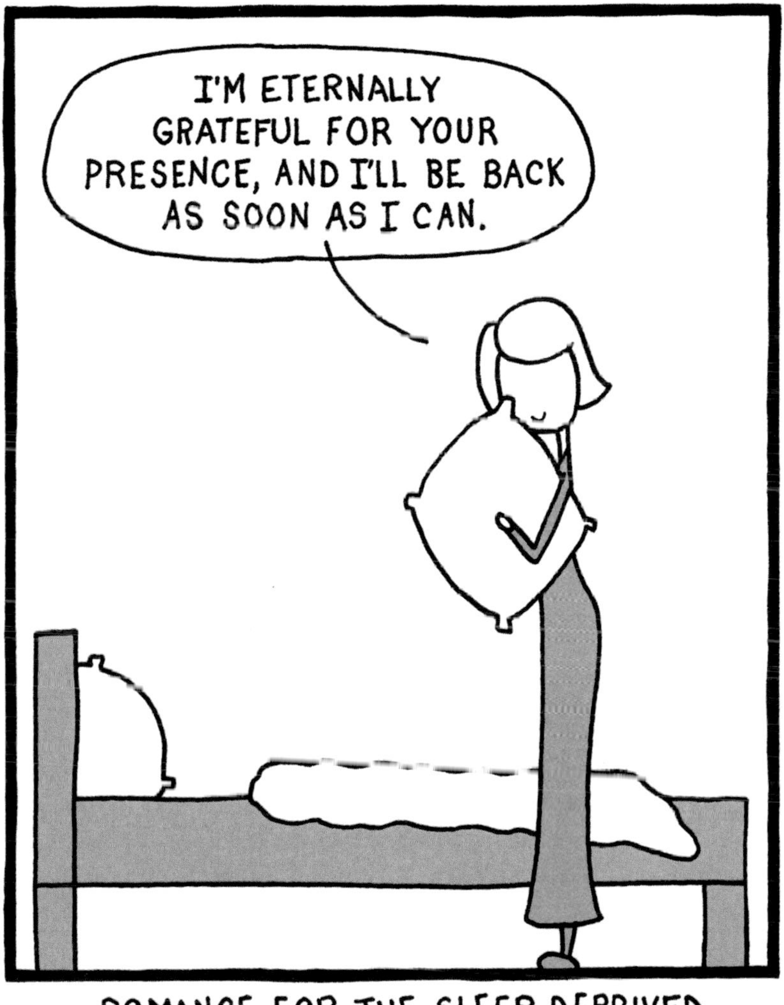
I'M ETERNALLY GRATEFUL FOR YOUR PRESENCE, AND I'LL BE BACK AS SOON AS I CAN.

ROMANCE FOR THE SLEEP DEPRIVED.

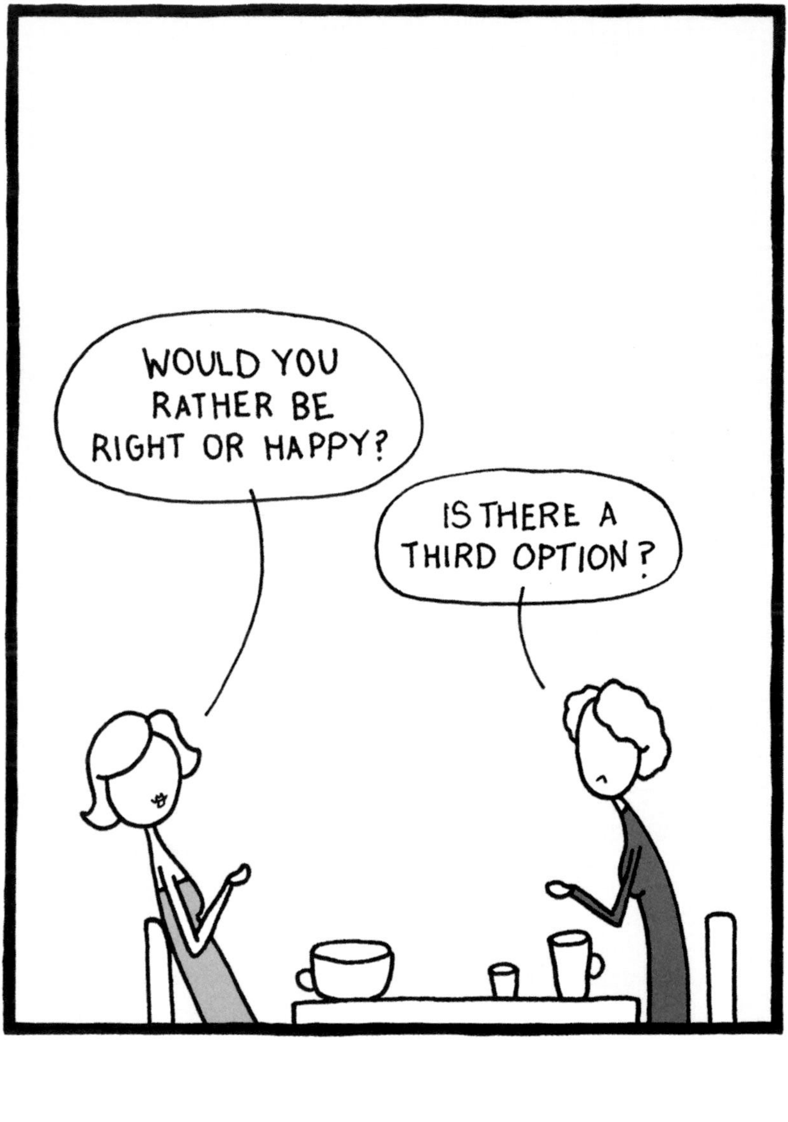
WOULD YOU RATHER BE RIGHT OR HAPPY?
IS THERE A THIRD OPTION?

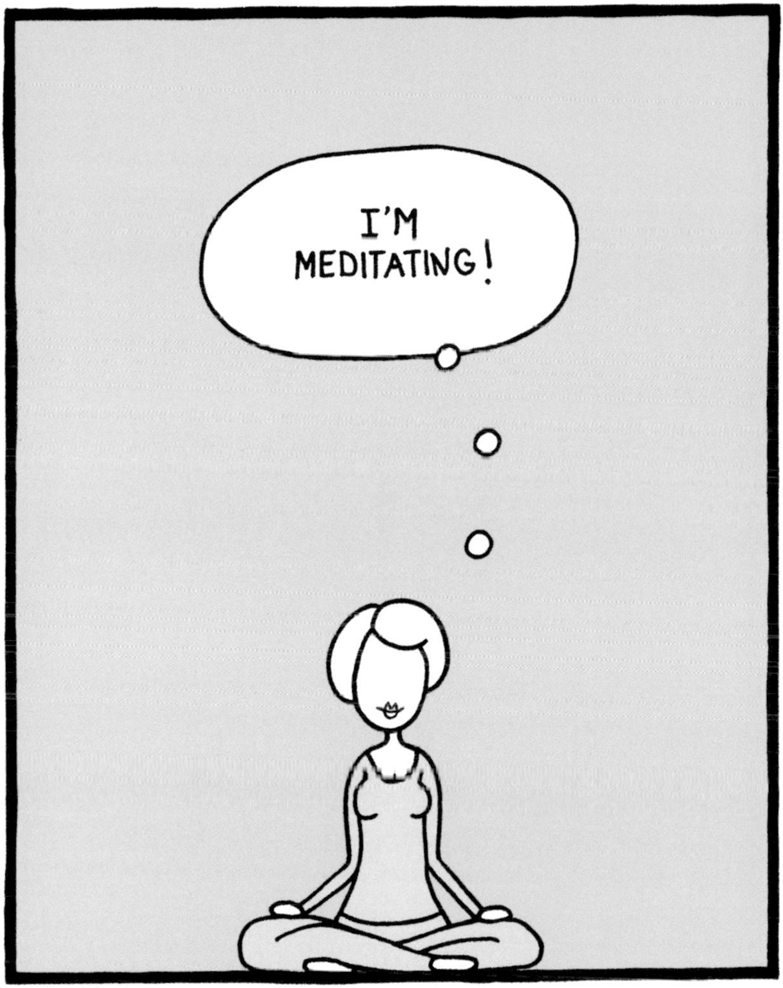
I'M MEDITATING!

WOMAN NOT MEDITATING.

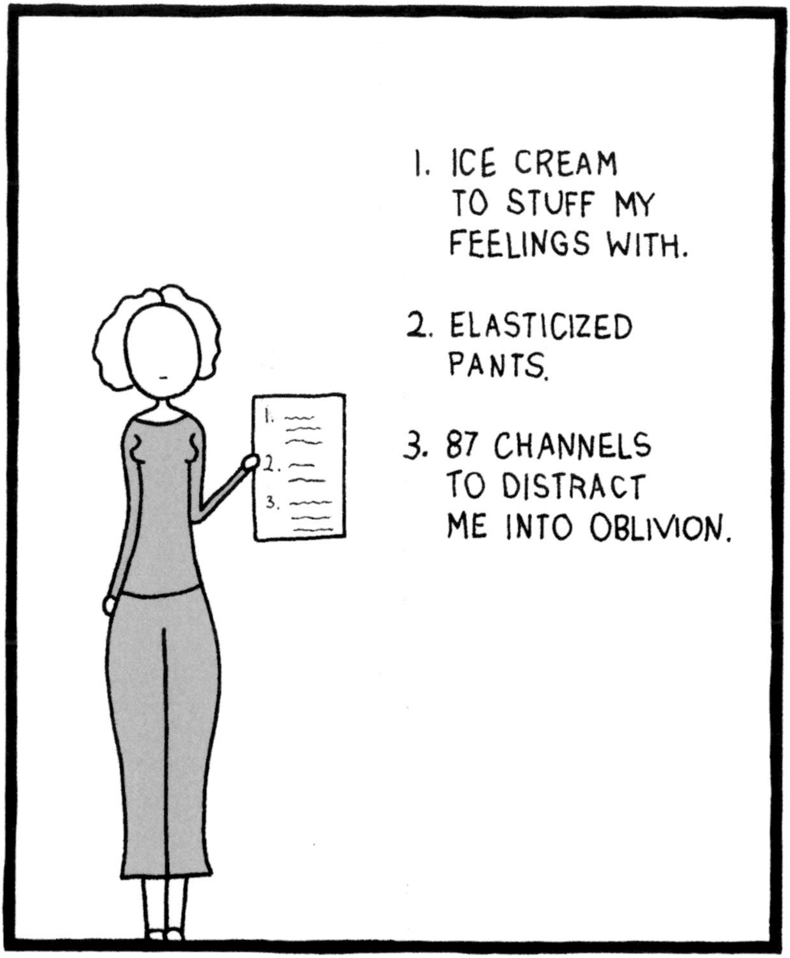
1. ICE CREAM TO STUFF MY FEELINGS WITH.
2. ELASTICIZED PANTS.
3. 87 CHANNELS TO DISTRACT ME INTO OBLIVION.

I WROTE MY GRATITUDE LIST, YET I STILL DON'T FEEL BETTER.

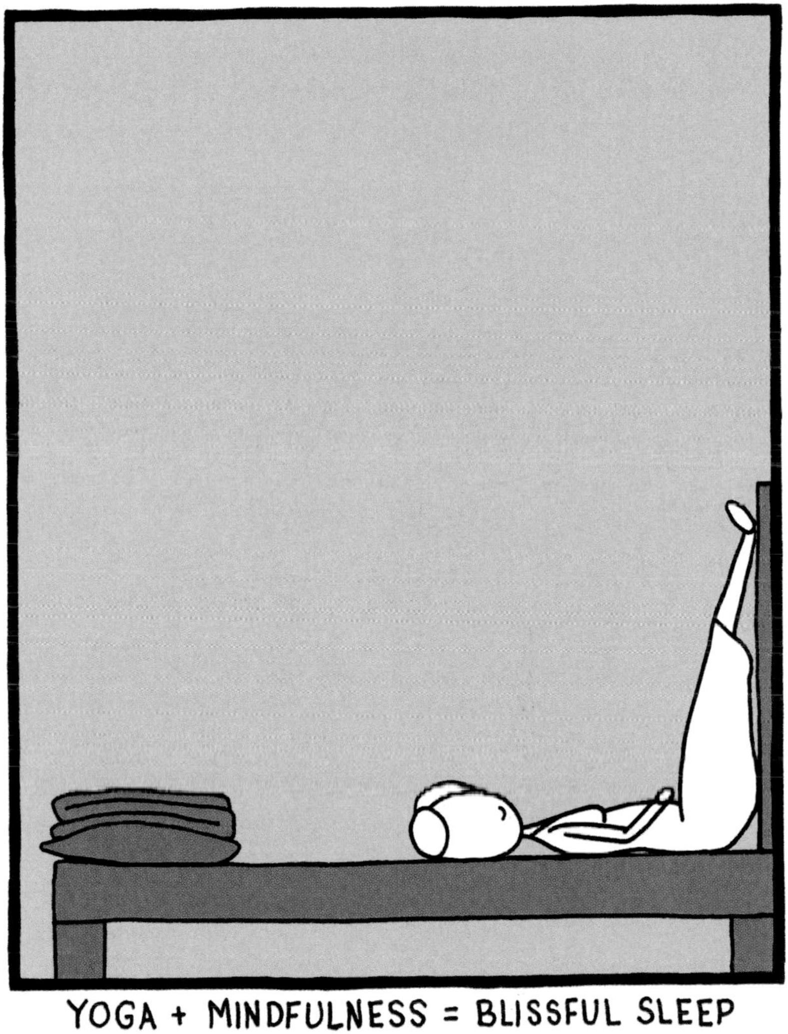

YOGA + MINDFULNESS = BLISSFUL SLEEP

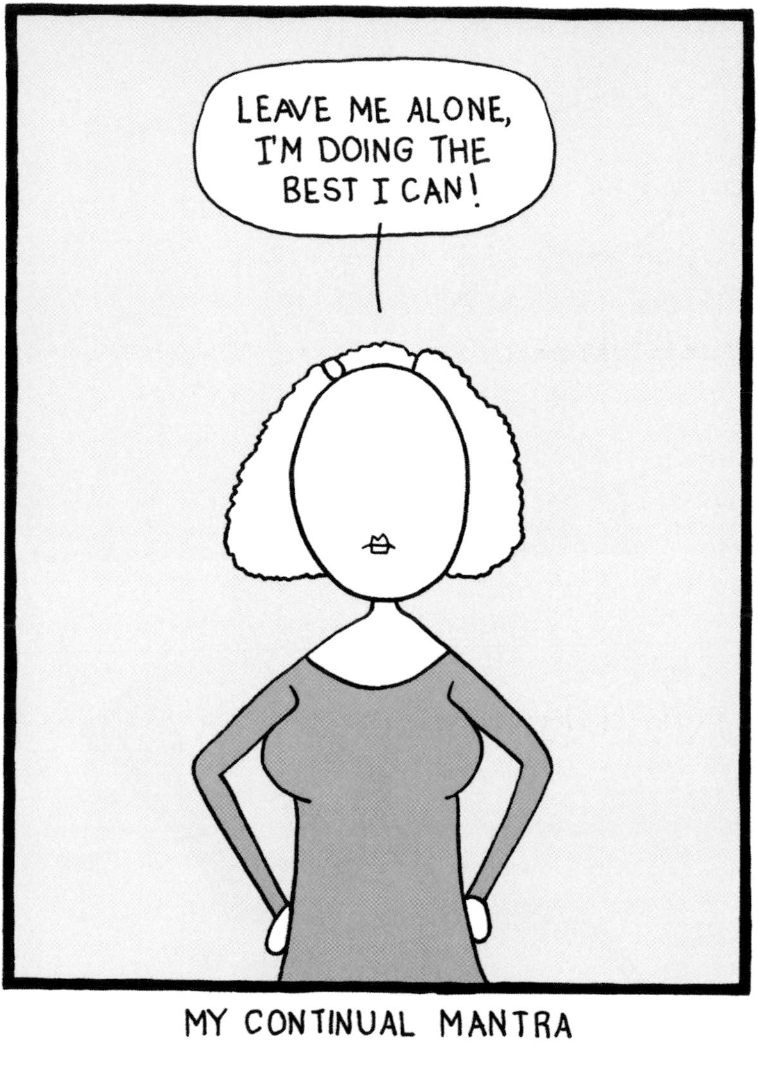
LEAVE ME ALONE, I'M DOING THE BEST I CAN!

MY CONTINUAL MANTRA

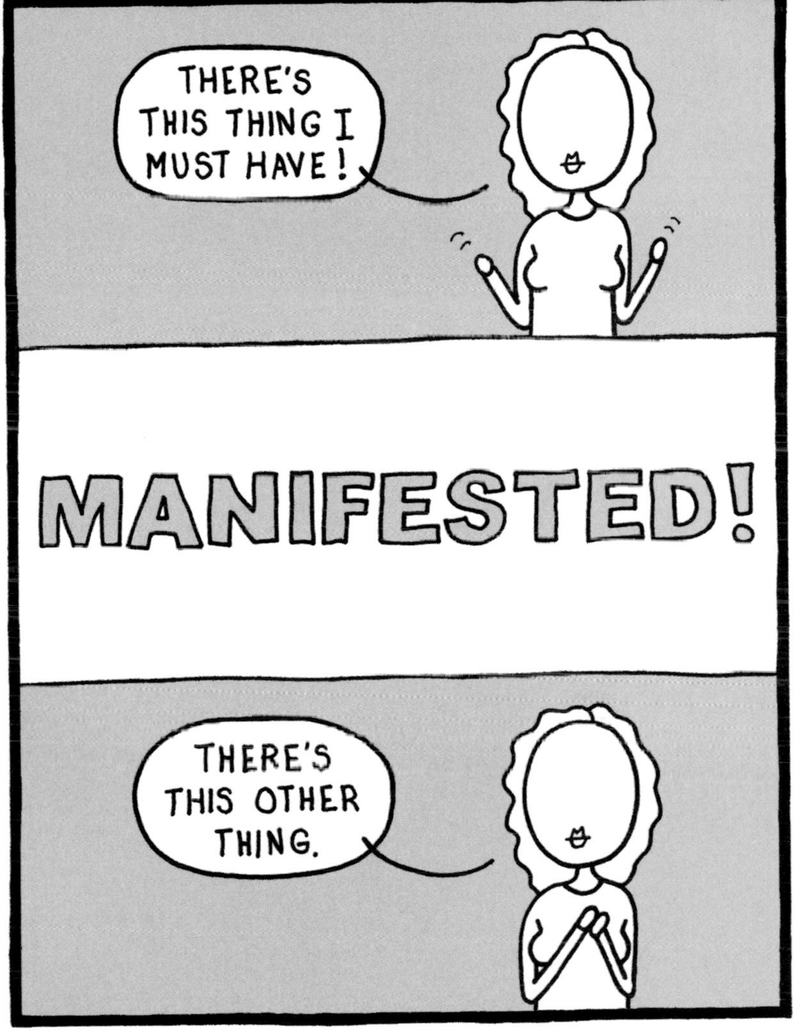
THERE'S THIS THING I MUST HAVE!
MANIFESTED!
THERE'S THIS OTHER THING.

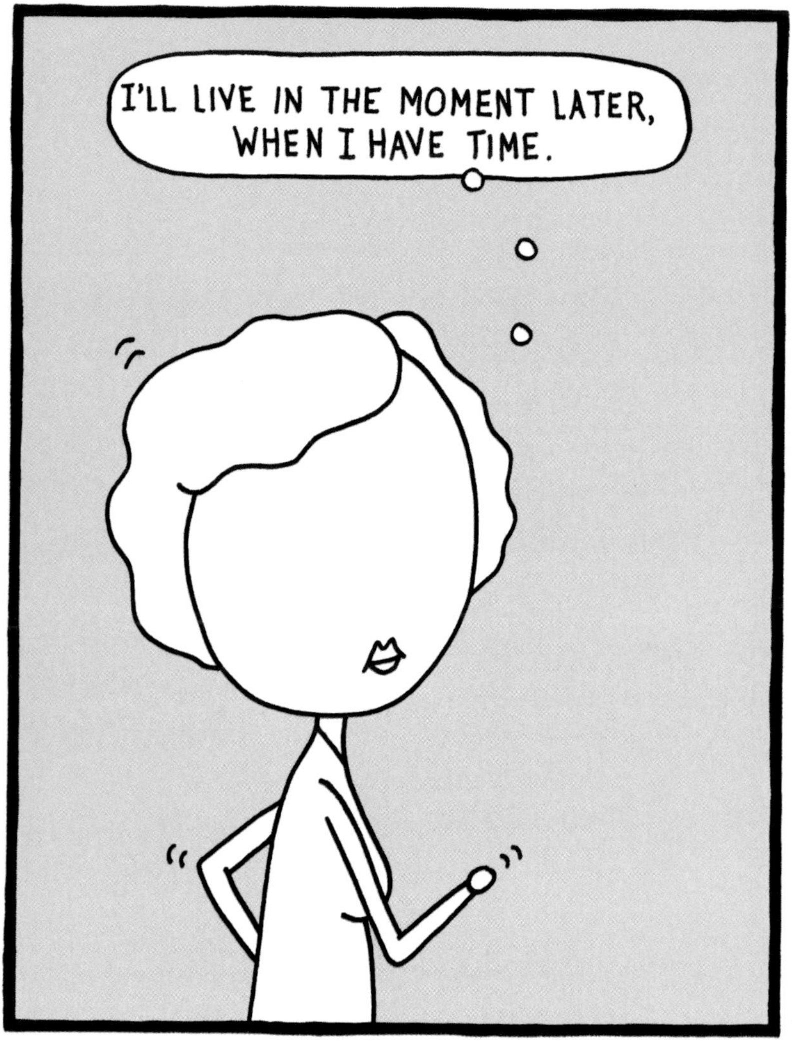
I'LL LIVE IN THE MOMENT LATER, WHEN I HAVE TIME.

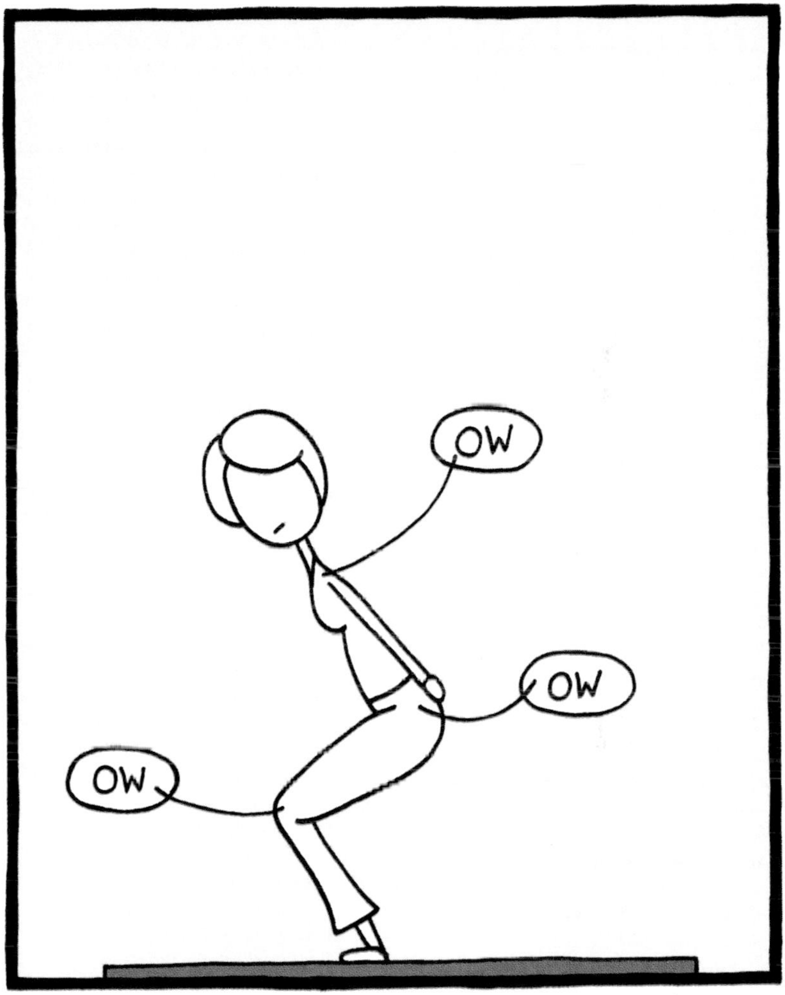
OW
OW
OW

YOGA BRINGS RELIEF, EVENTUALLY.

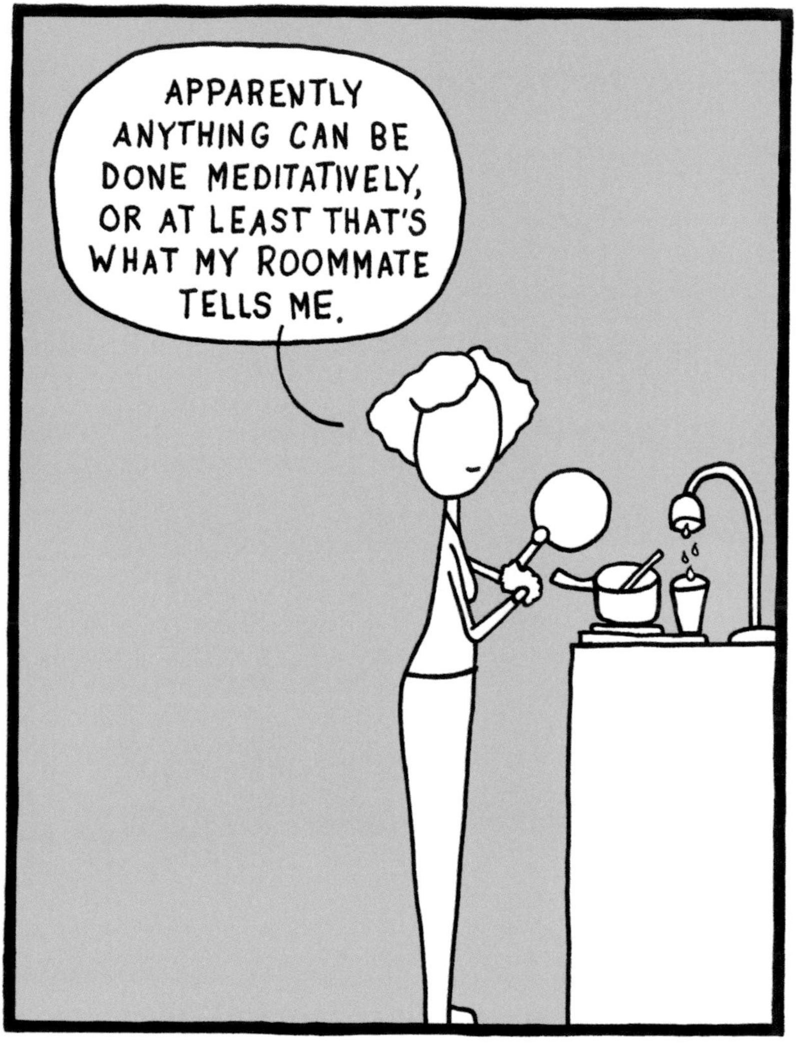
APPARENTLY ANYTHING CAN BE DONE MEDITATIVELY, OR AT LEAST THAT'S WHAT MY ROOMMATE TELLS ME.

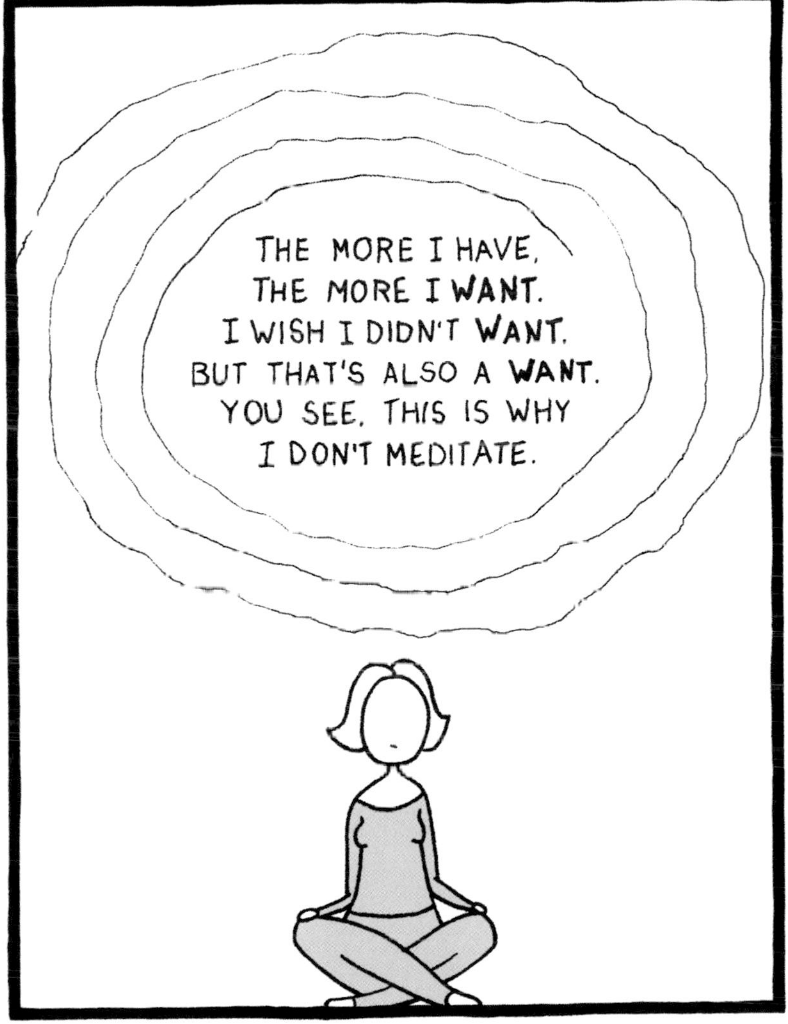
THE MORE I HAVE,
THE MORE I **WANT**.
I WISH I DIDN'T **WANT**.
BUT THAT'S ALSO A **WANT**.
YOU SEE, THIS IS WHY
I DON'T MEDITATE.

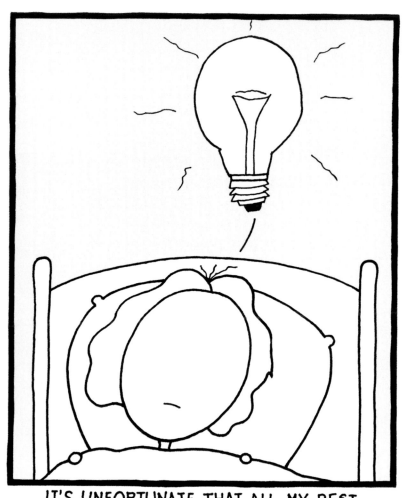

IT'S UNFORTUNATE THAT ALL MY BEST
THINKING HAPPENS AFTER MIDNIGHT.

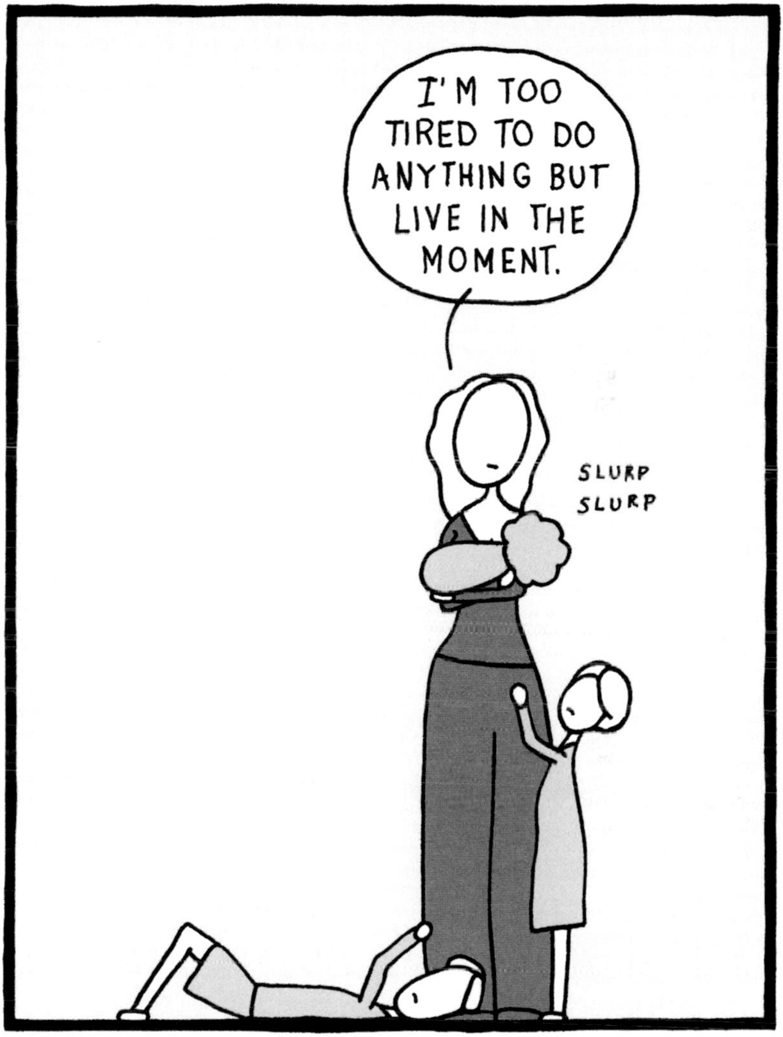
I'M TOO TIRED TO DO ANYTHING BUT LIVE IN THE MOMENT.
SLURP
SLURP

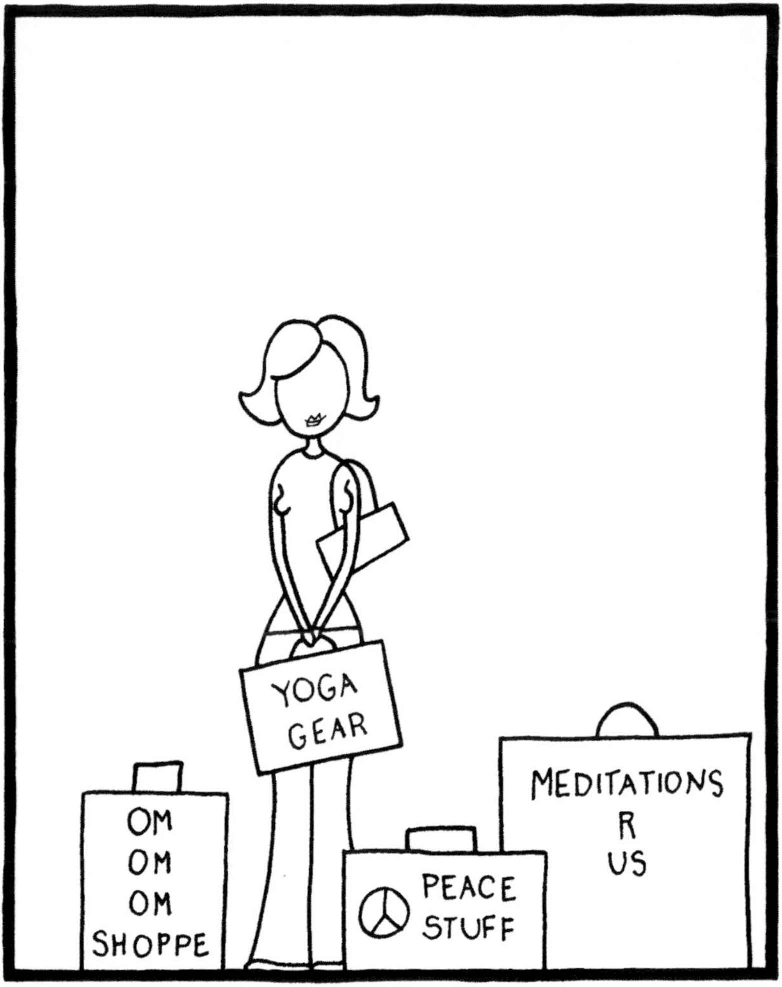
YOGA
GEAR
OM
OM
OM
SHOPPE
PEACE
STUFF
MEDITATIONS
R
US

OBTAINING THE HIGHEST LEVEL OF AVOIDANCE.

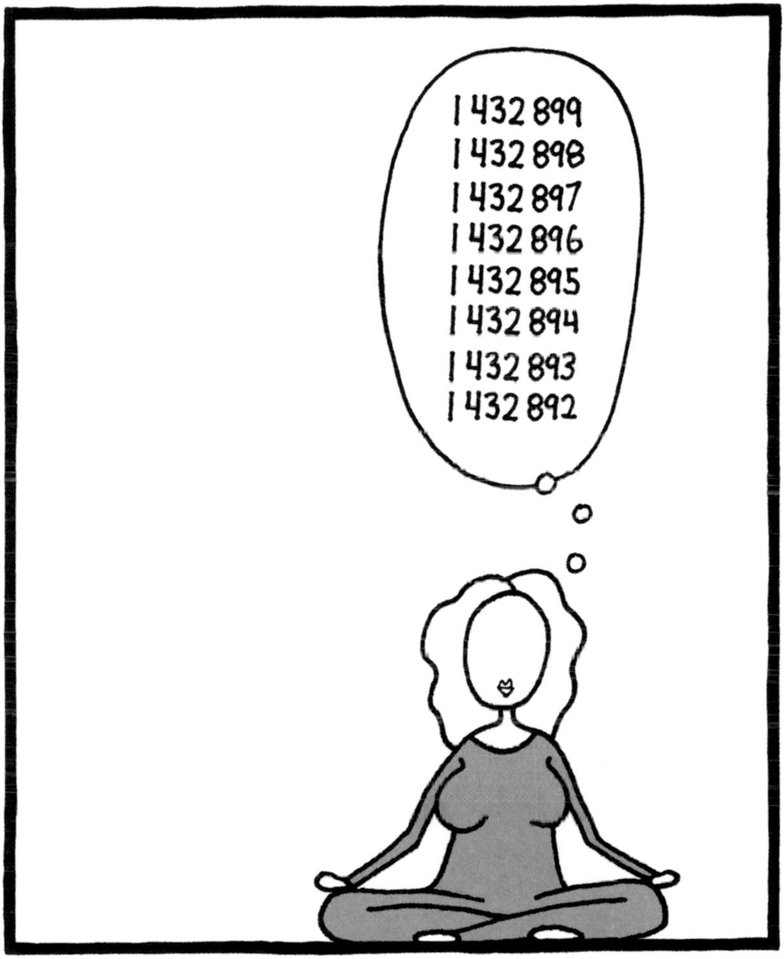
1 432 899
1 432 898
1 432 897
1 432 896
1 432 895
1 432 894
1 432 893
1 432 892

TRICKING THE BRAIN INTO LETTING THE MIND MEDITATE.

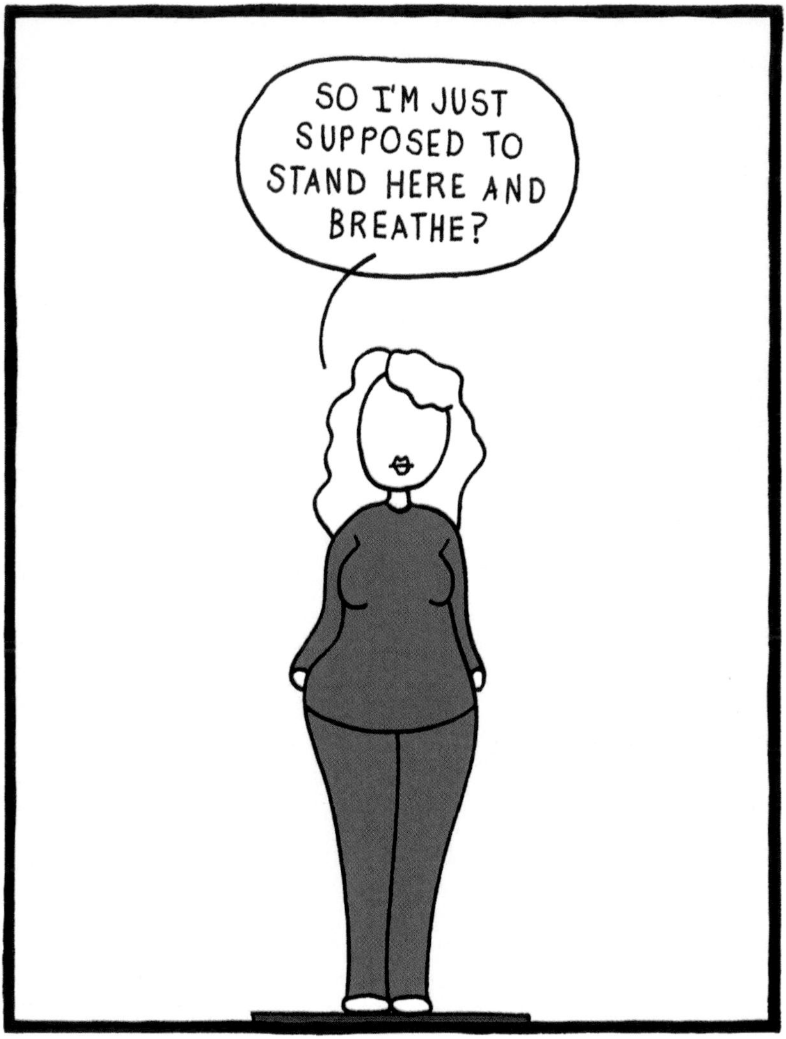
SO I'M JUST SUPPOSED TO STAND HERE AND BREATHE?

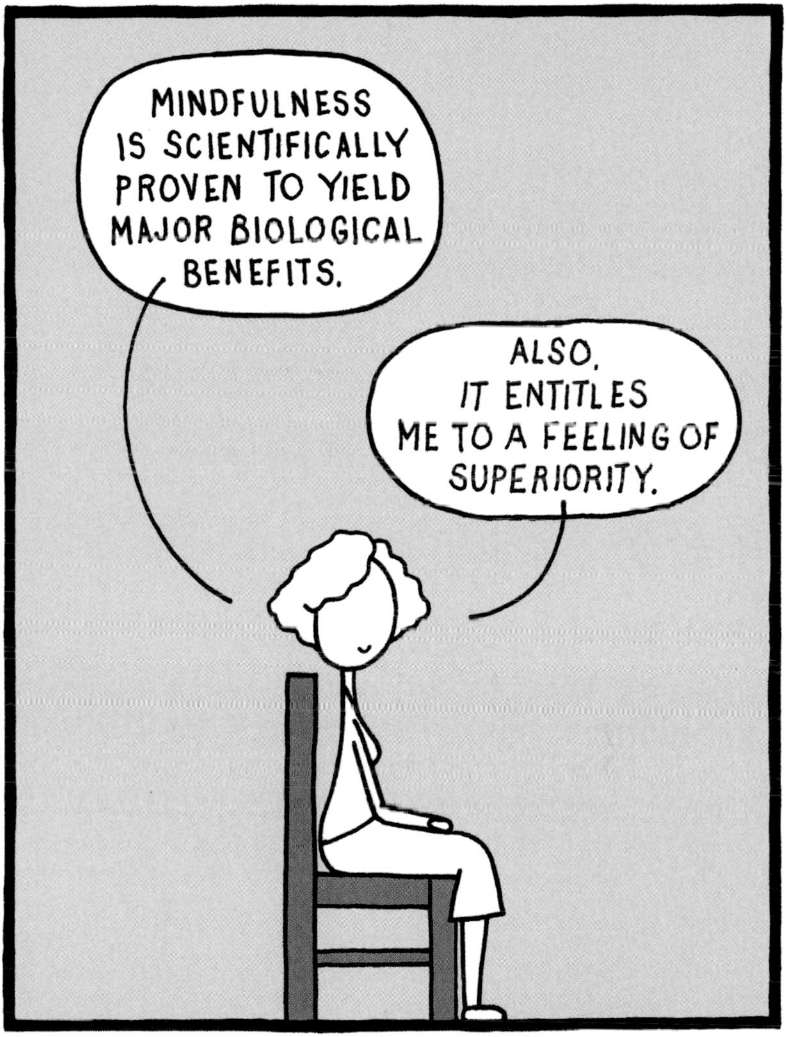
MINDFULNESS IS SCIENTIFICALLY PROVEN TO YIELD MAJOR BIOLOGICAL BENEFITS.
ALSO, IT ENTITLES ME TO A FEELING OF SUPERIORITY.

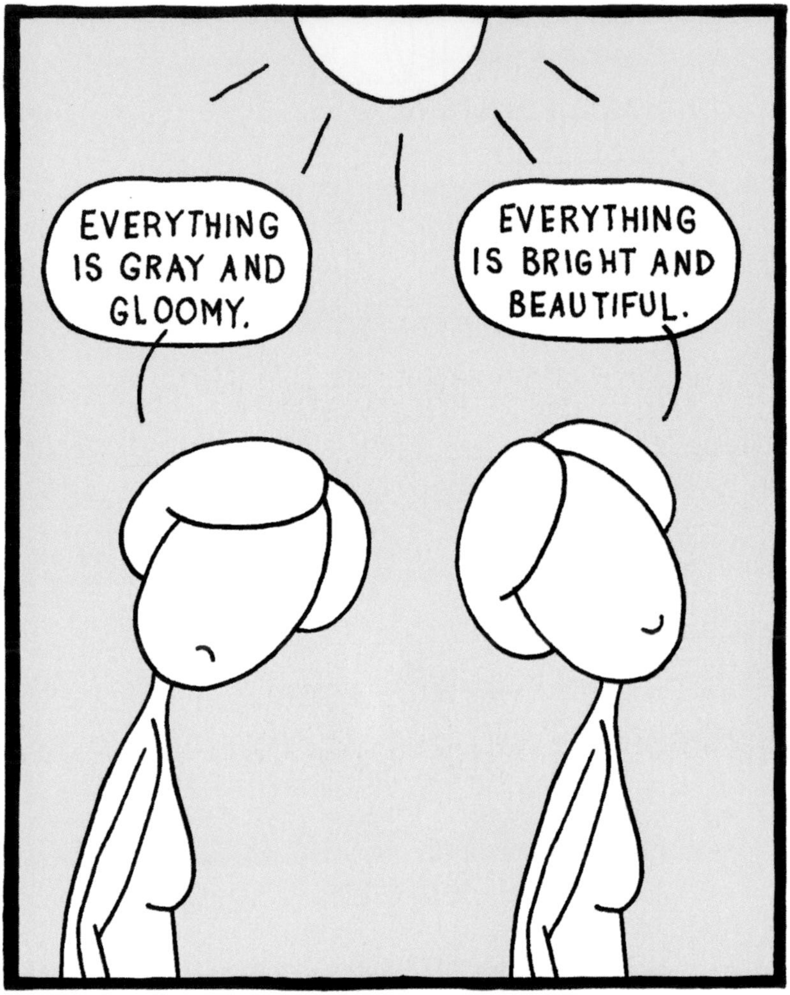
EVERYTHING IS GRAY AND GLOOMY.
EVERYTHING IS BRIGHT AND BEAUTIFUL.

PERSPECTIVE IS EVERYTHING.

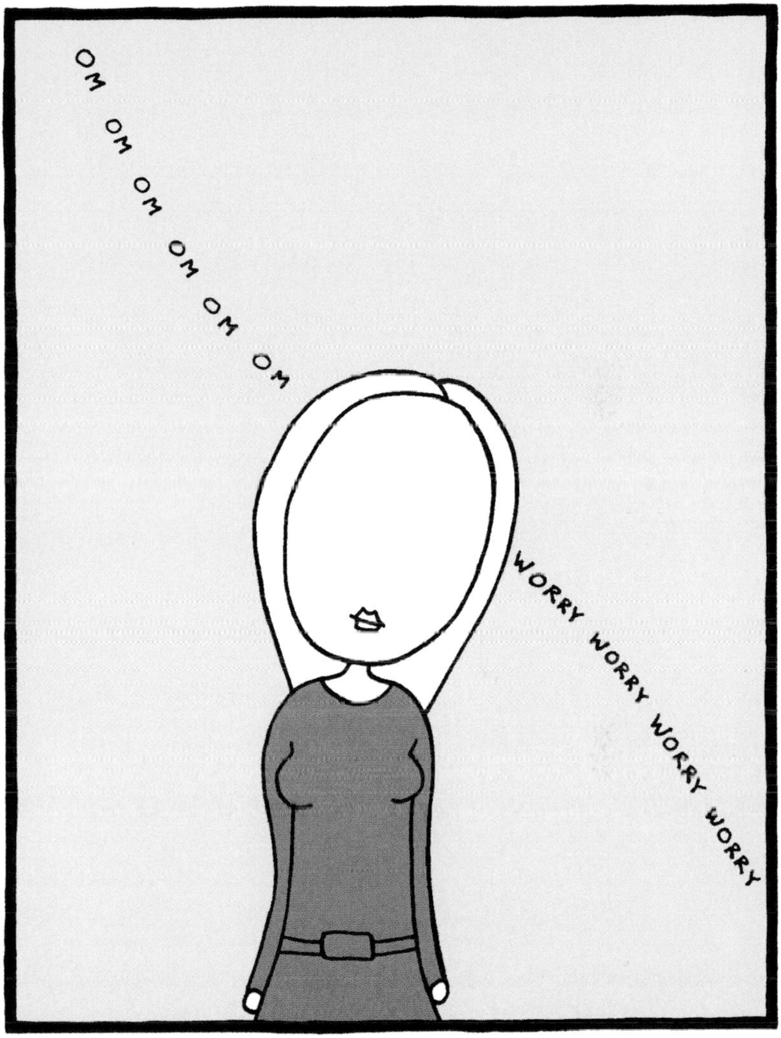
OM OM OM OM OM OM
WORRY WORRY WORRY WORRY

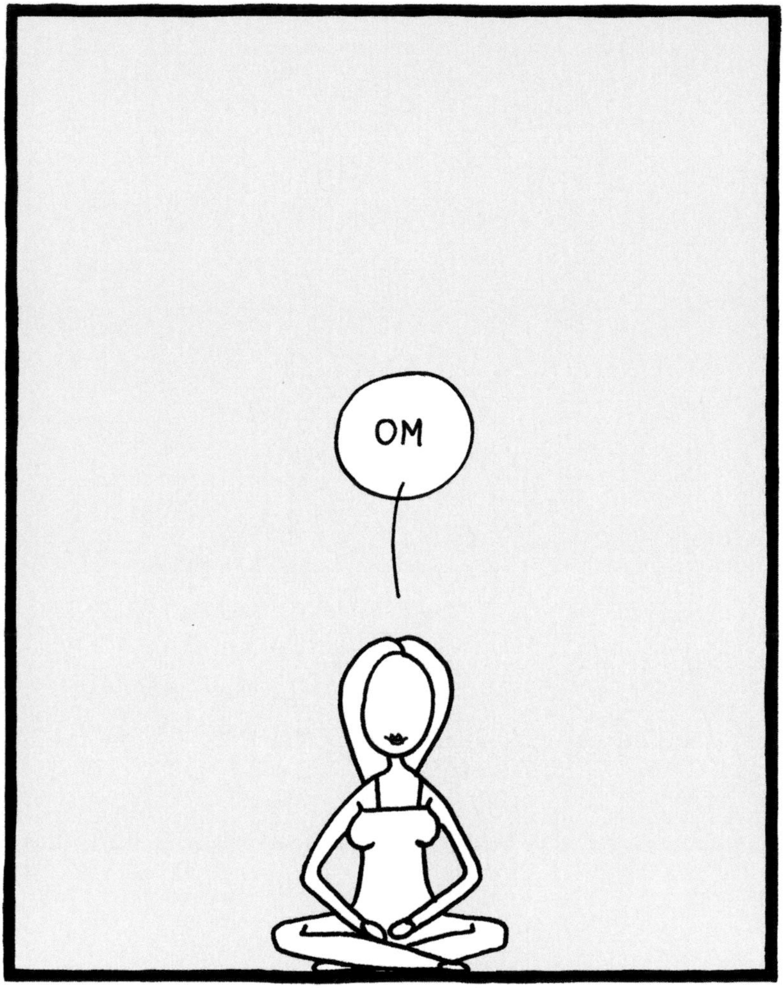
OM
CREATIVE PROCRASTINATION.

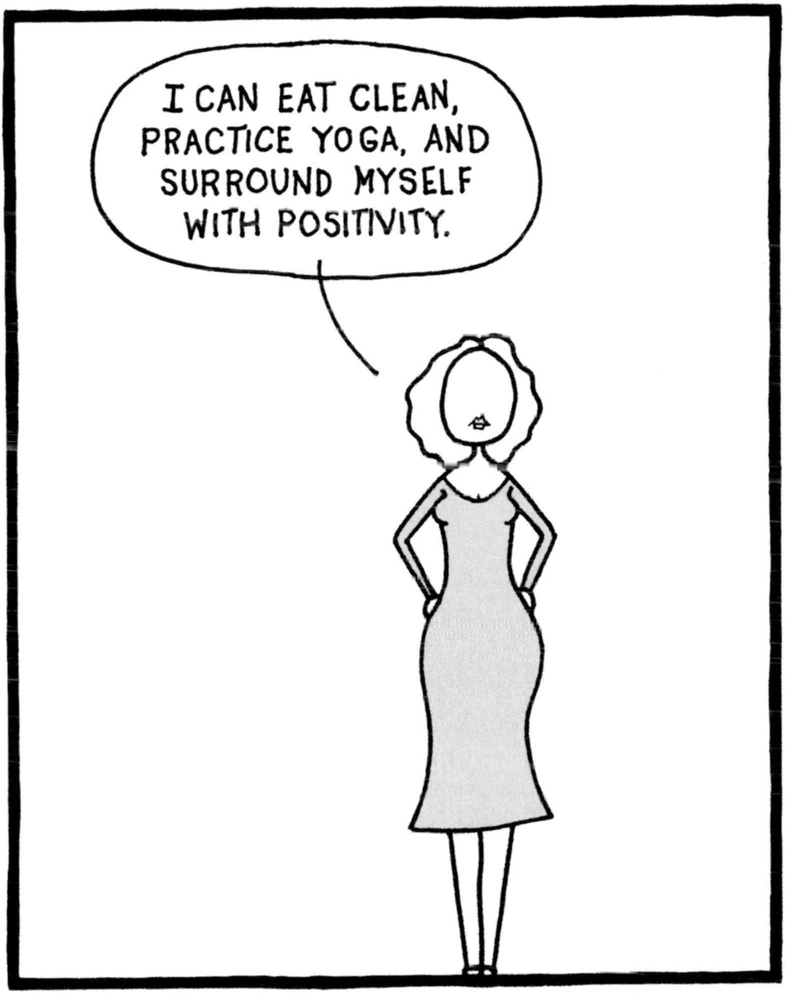
I CAN EAT CLEAN, PRACTICE YOGA, AND SURROUND MYSELF WITH POSITIVITY.

I JUST CAN'T DO IT ALL AT ONCE.

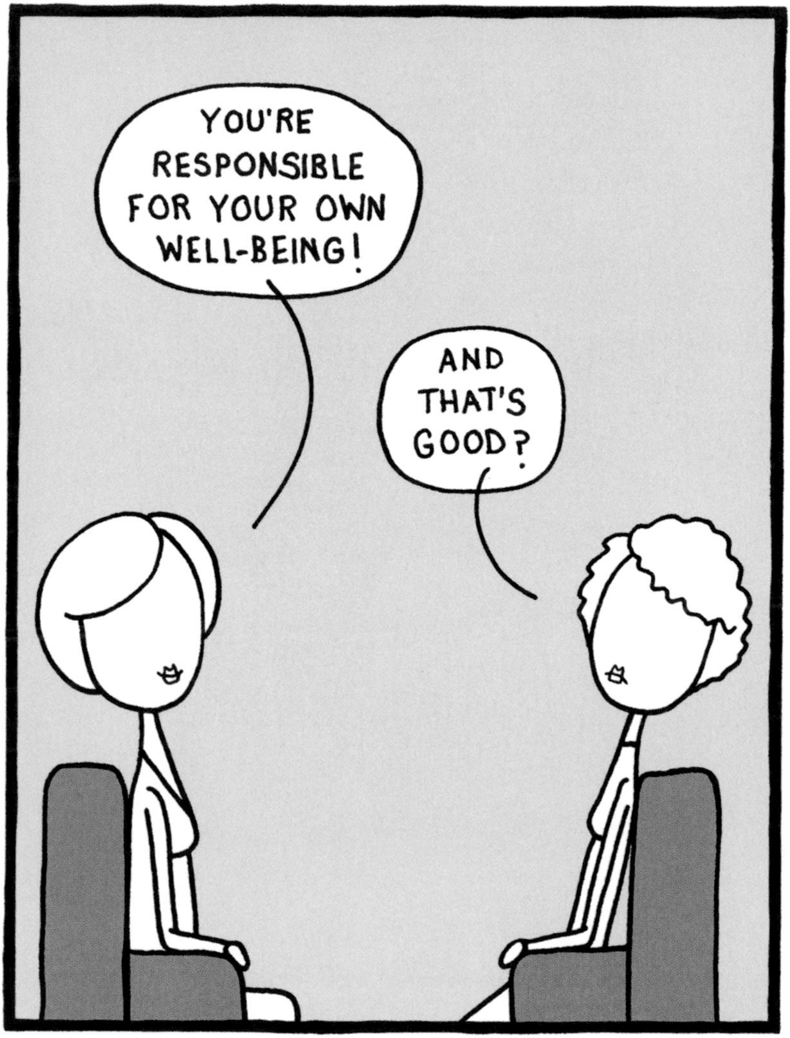
YOU'RE RESPONSIBLE FOR YOUR OWN WELL-BEING!
AND THAT'S GOOD?

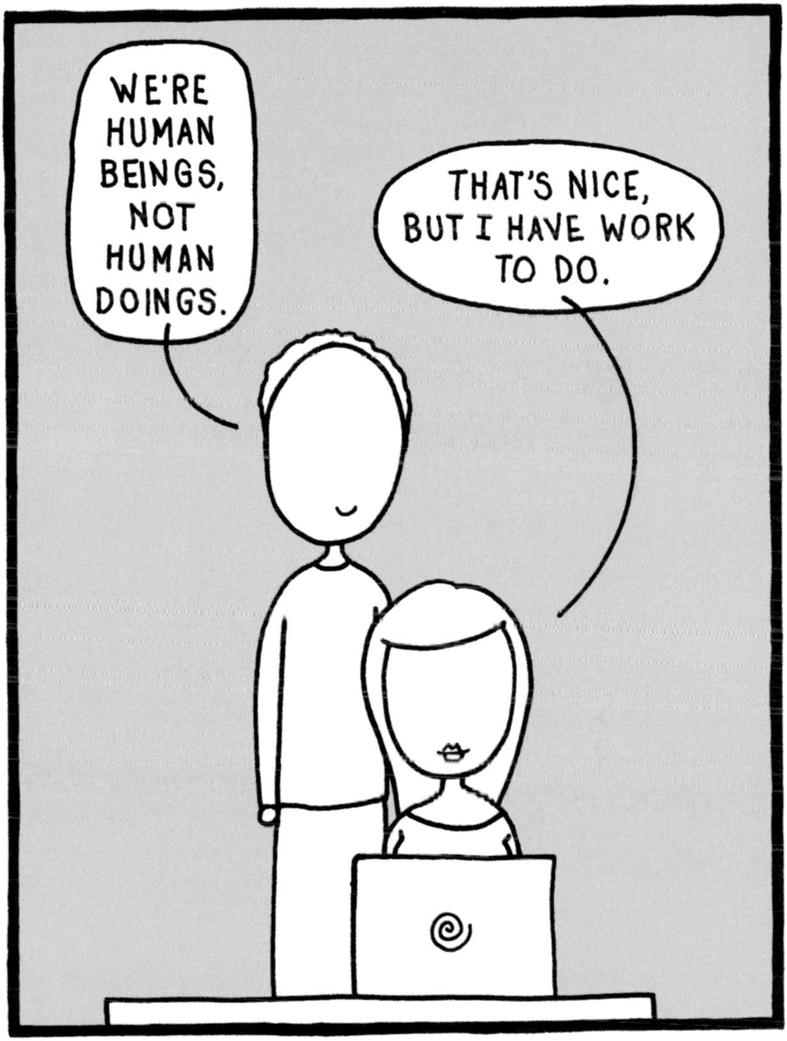
WE'RE HUMAN BEINGS, NOT HUMAN DOINGS.
THAT'S NICE, BUT I HAVE WORK TO DO.

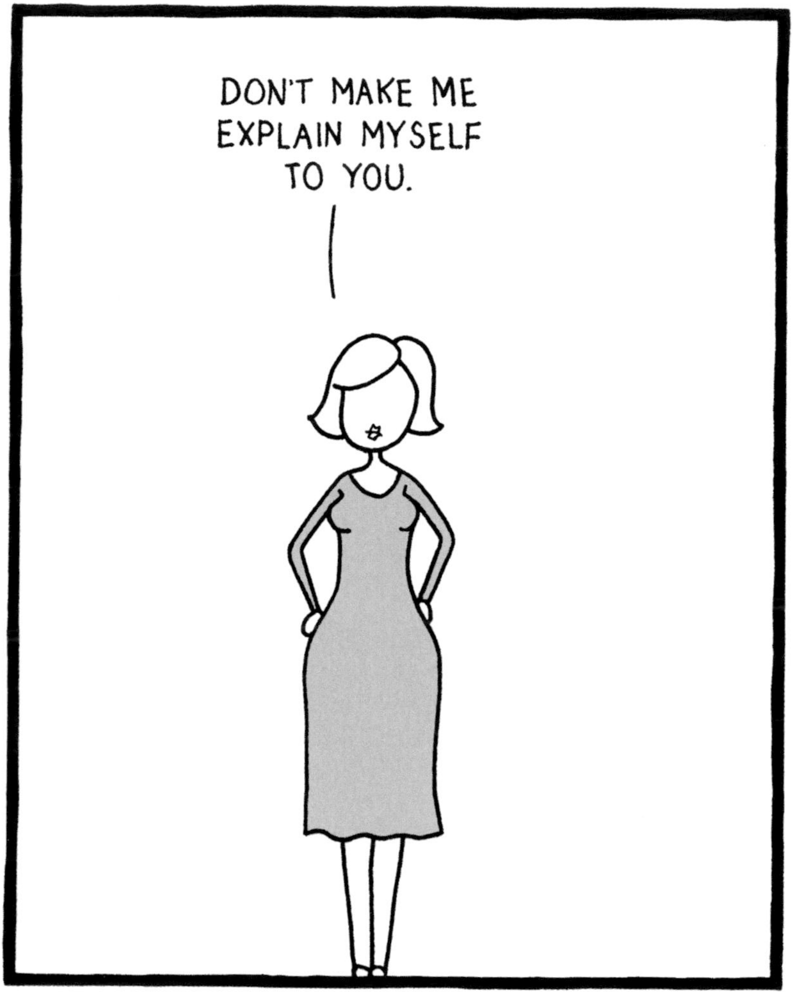
DON'T MAKE ME EXPLAIN MYSELF TO YOU.

AS IS, I BARELY KNOW MYSELF.

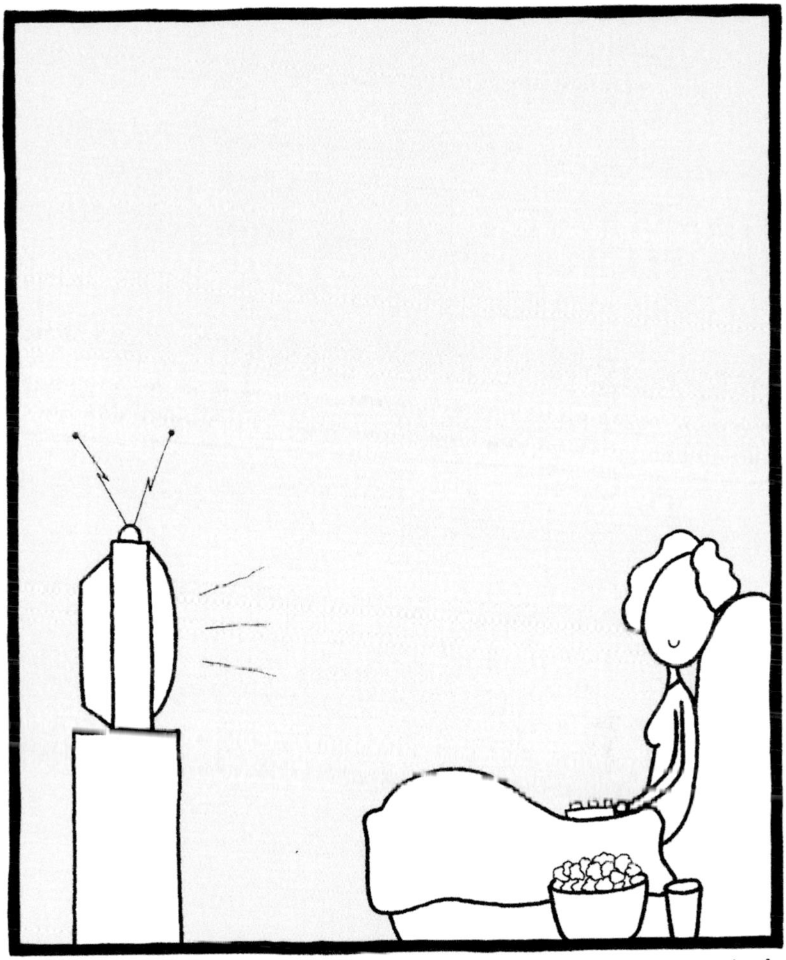

I LIKE RERUNS - IT'S THE ONLY TIME I'M CERTAIN ABOUT WHAT THE FUTURE WILL BRING.

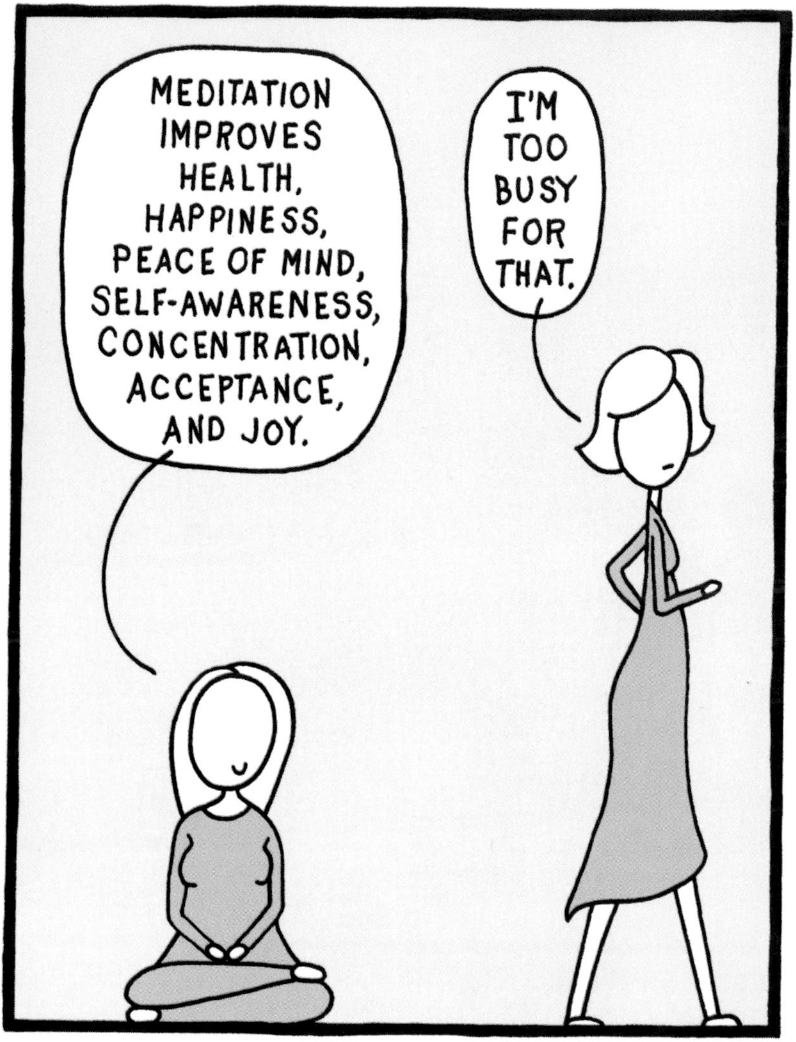
MEDITATION IMPROVES HEALTH, HAPPINESS, PEACE OF MIND, SELF-AWARENESS, CONCENTRATION, ACCEPTANCE, AND JOY.
I'M TOO BUSY FOR THAT.

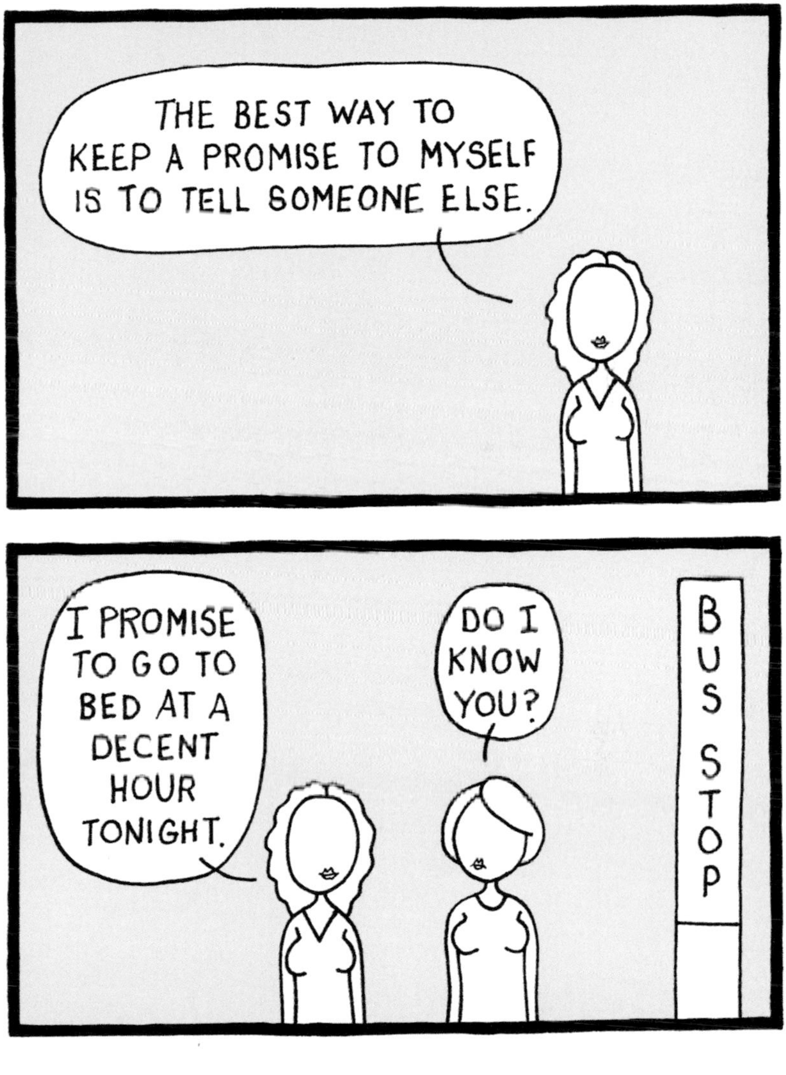
THE BEST WAY TO KEEP A PROMISE TO MYSELF IS TO TELL SOMEONE ELSE.
I PROMISE TO GO TO BED AT A DECENT HOUR TONIGHT.
DO I KNOW YOU?
BUS STOP

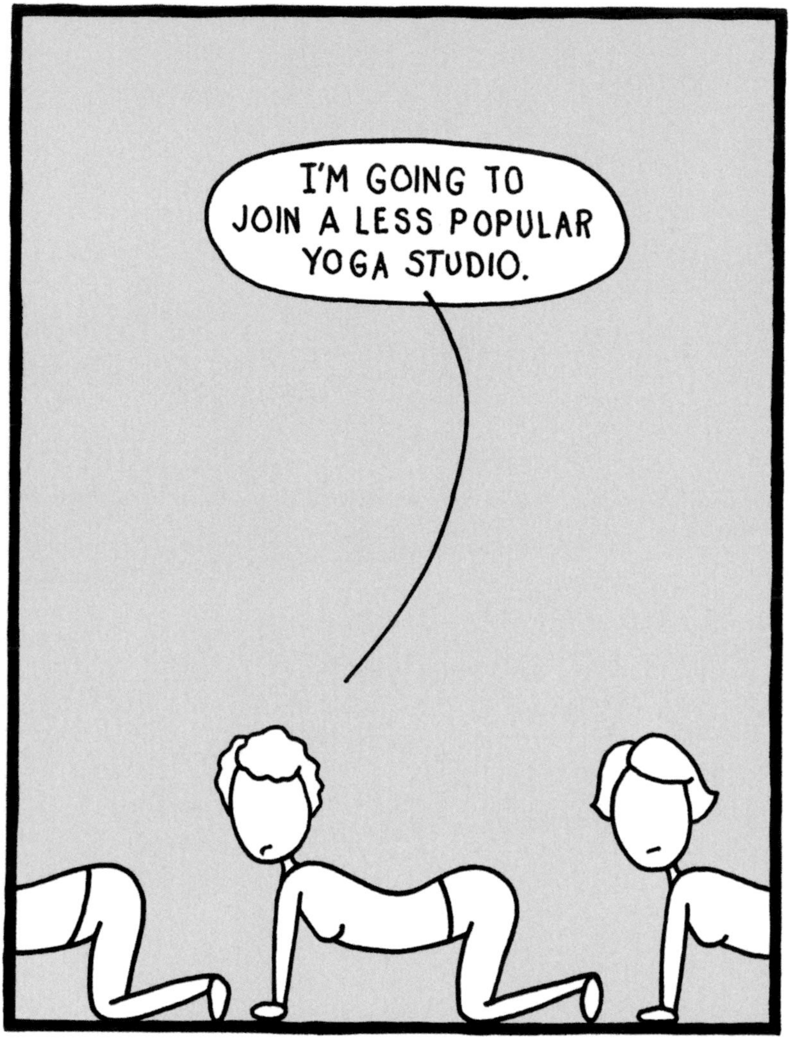
I'M GOING TO JOIN A LESS POPULAR YOGA STUDIO.

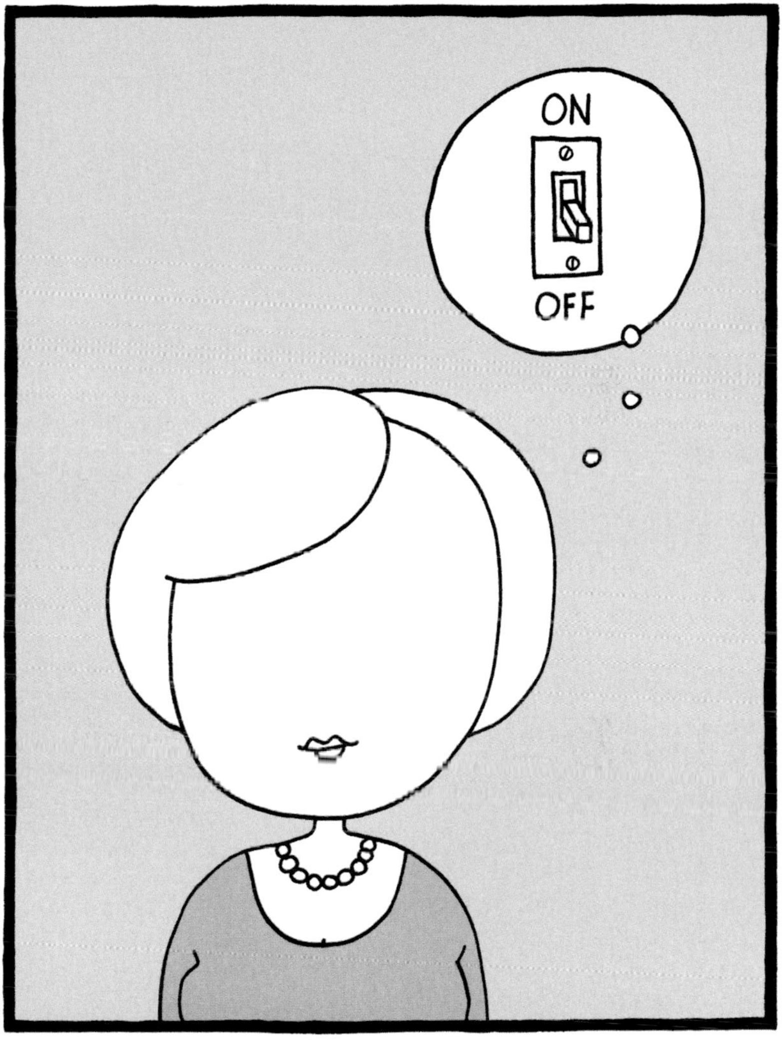
ON
OFF

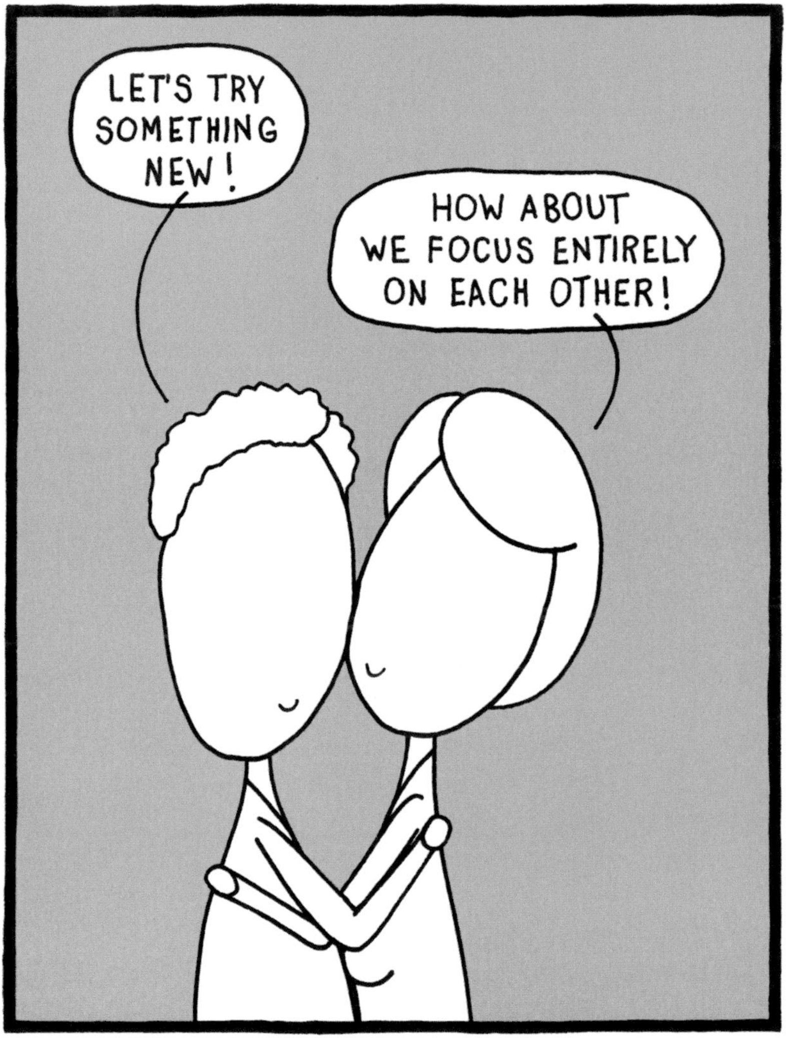
LET'S TRY SOMETHING NEW!
HOW ABOUT WE FOCUS ENTIRELY ON EACH OTHER!

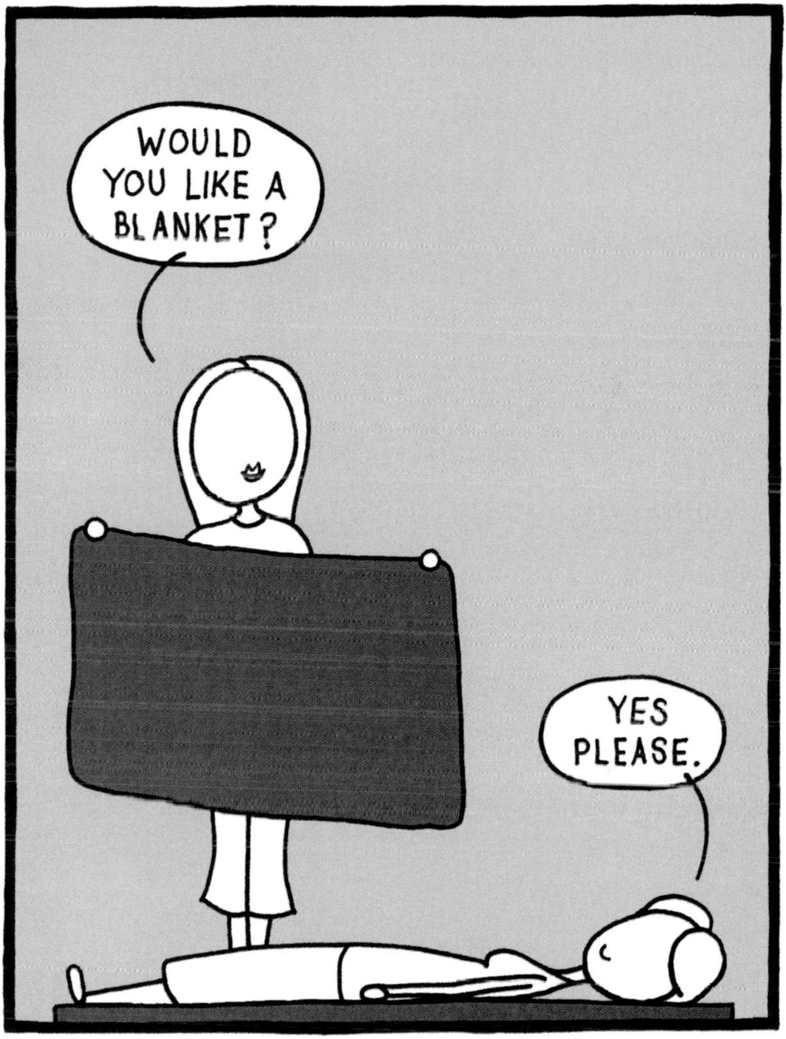
WOULD YOU LIKE A BLANKET?
YES PLEASE.

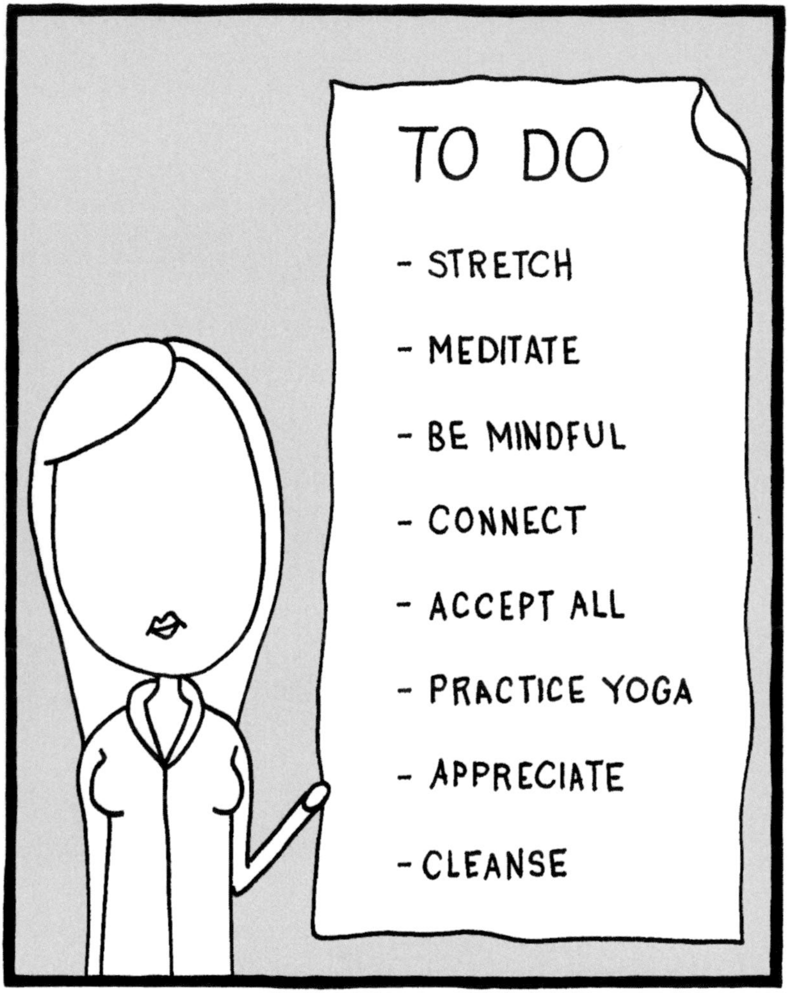
TO DO
- STRETCH
- MEDITATE
- BE MINDFUL
- CONNECT
- ACCEPT ALL
- PRACTICE YOGA
- APPRECIATE
- CLEANSE

TOO MUCH TO DO TO JUST BE.

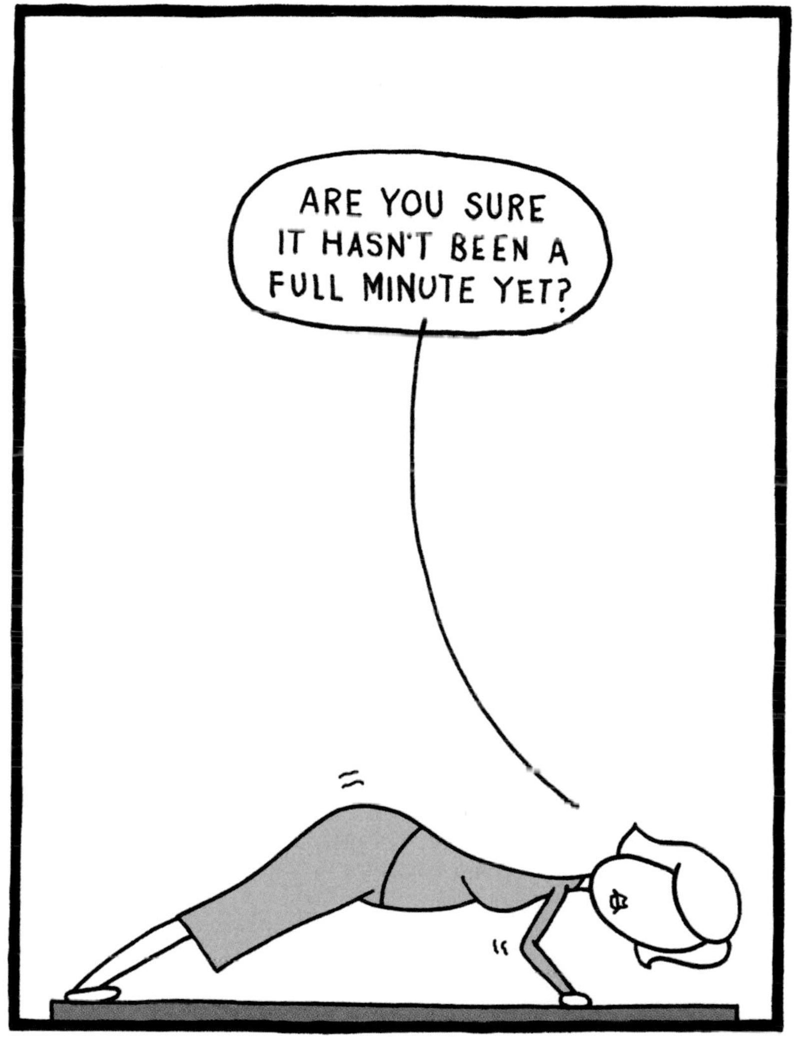
ARE YOU SURE IT HASN'T BEEN A FULL MINUTE YET?

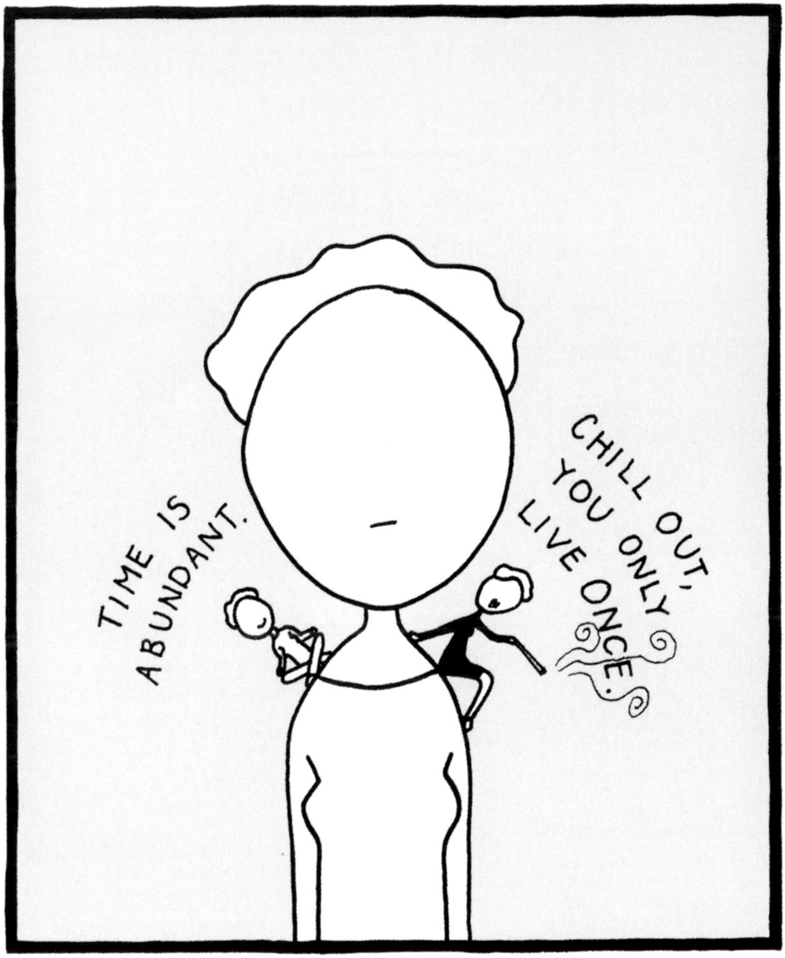
TIME IS ABUNDANT.
CHILL OUT, YOU ONLY LIVE ONCE.

EVEN THEY AGREE THAT I NEED TO RELAX.

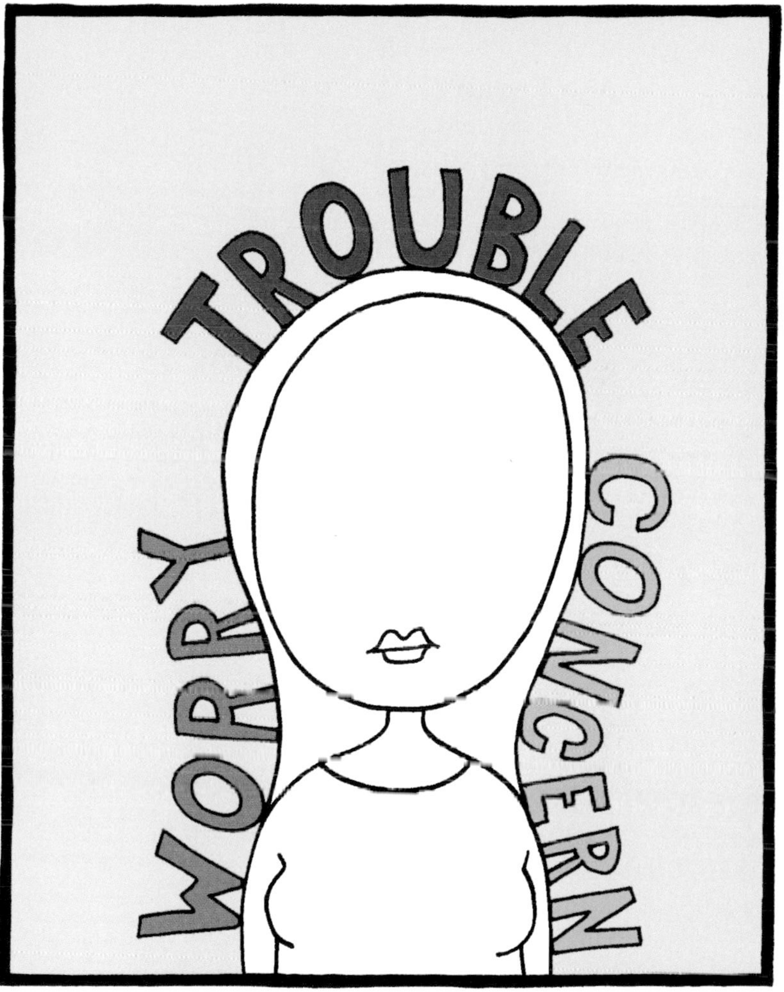
WORRY
TROUBLE
CONCERN

WHEN PROBLEMS HAVE PROBLEMS DETACHING.

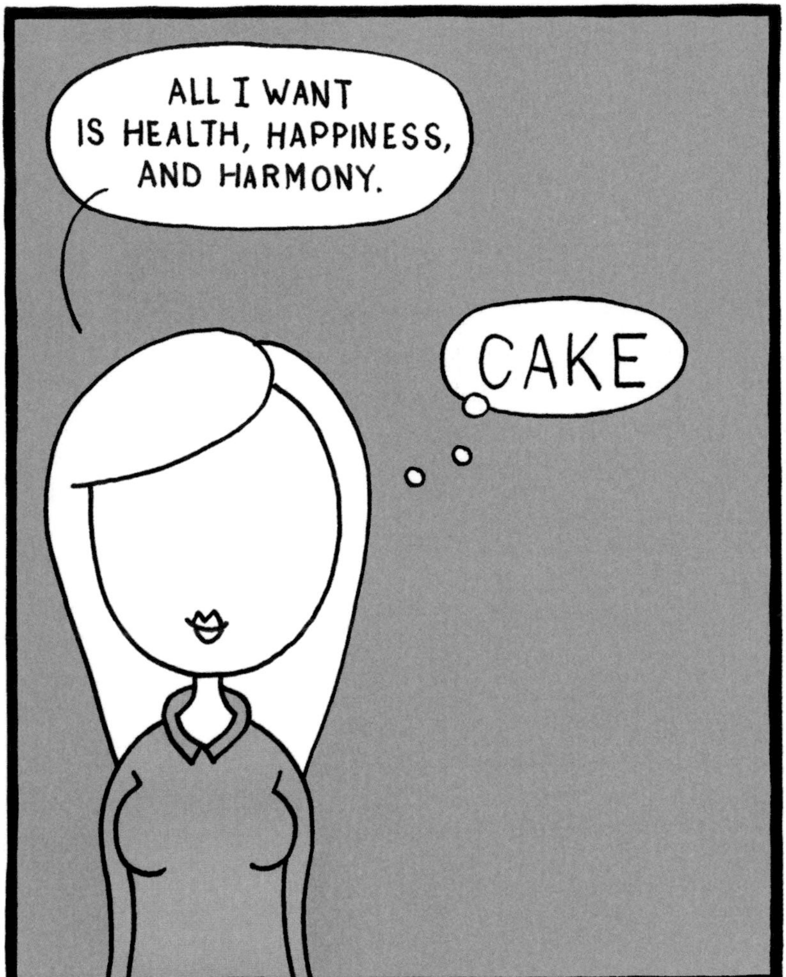
ALL I WANT IS HEALTH, HAPPINESS, AND HARMONY.
CAKE

THOUGHT TRUMPS TALK

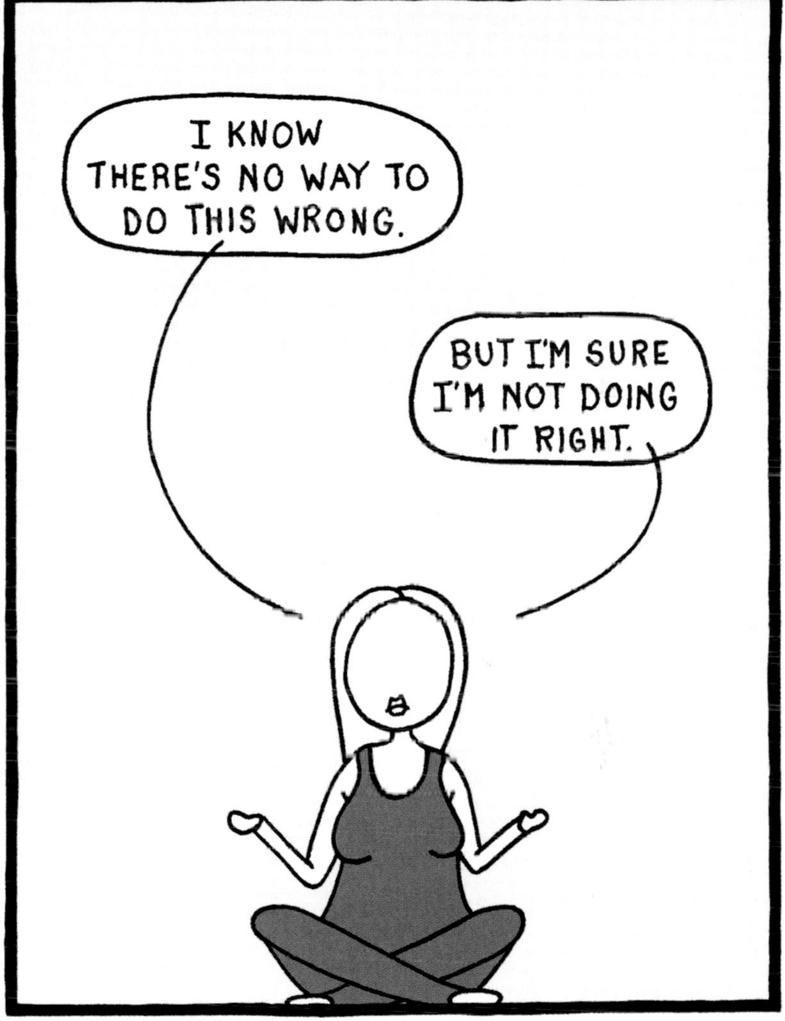
I KNOW THERE'S NO WAY TO DO THIS WRONG.
BUT I'M SURE I'M NOT DOING IT RIGHT.

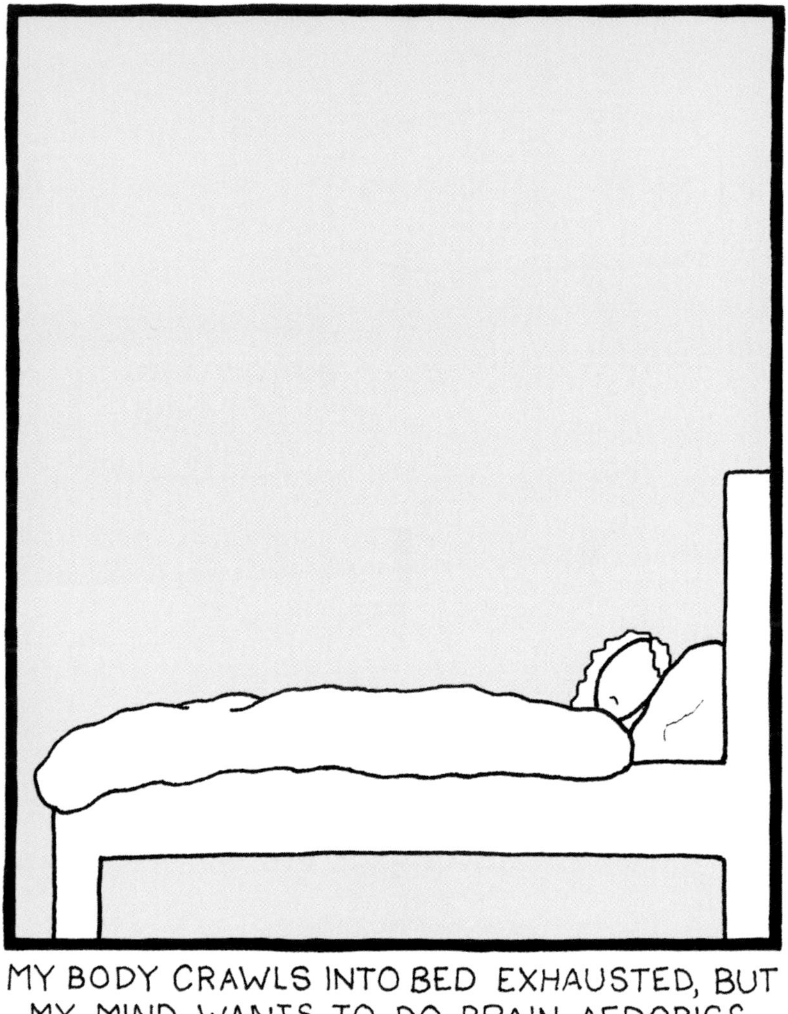

MY BODY CRAWLS INTO BED EXHAUSTED, BUT MY MIND WANTS TO DO BRAIN AEROBICS.

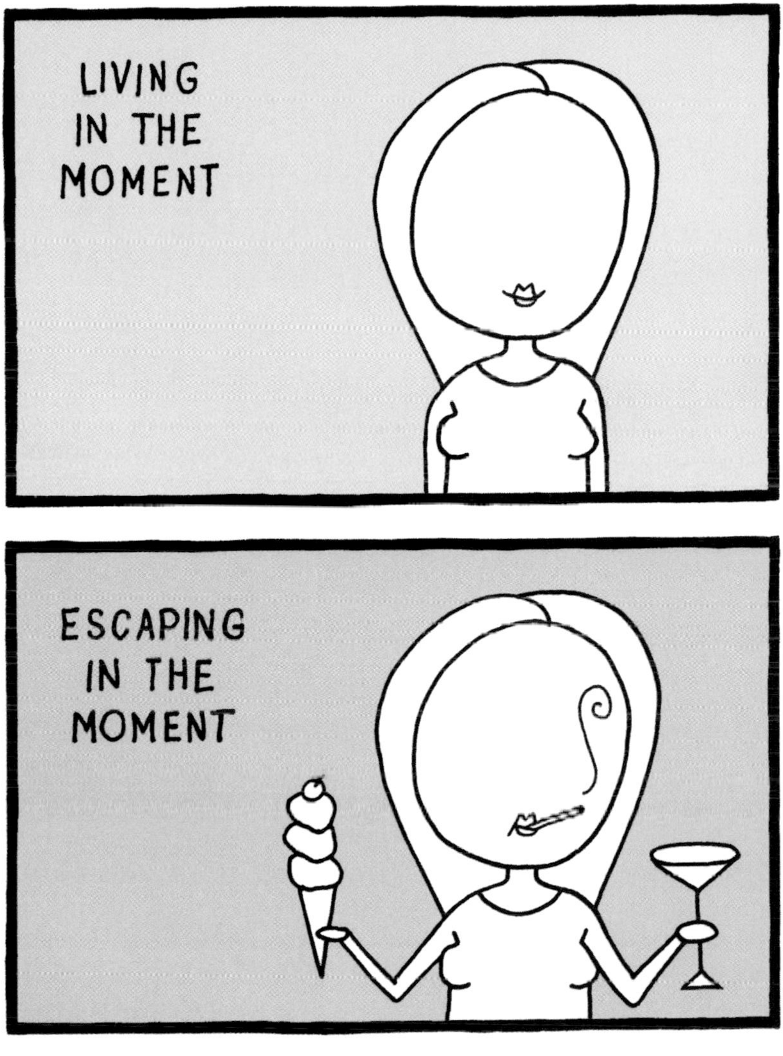
LIVING IN THE MOMENT
ESCAPING IN THE MOMENT

BUT IF I LET GO OF MY ANGER, THEN I'LL LOSE
THE ONLY CONNECTION I HAVE TO MY EX.

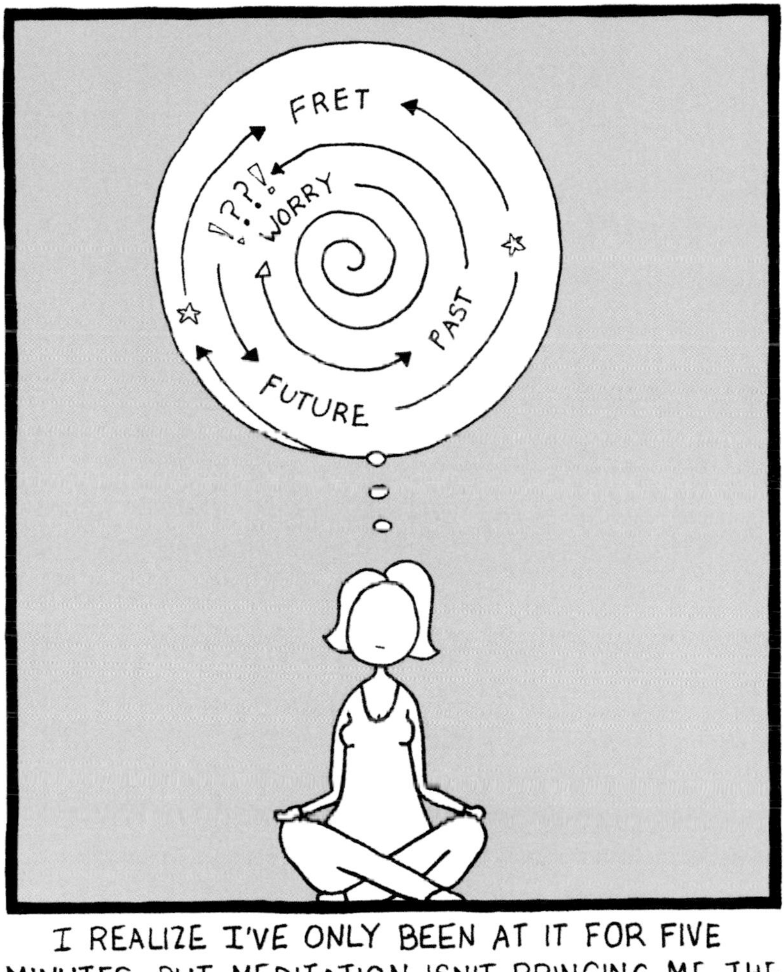
FRET
WORRY
!??!
PAST
FUTURE

I REALIZE I'VE ONLY BEEN AT IT FOR FIVE MINUTES, BUT MEDITATION ISN'T BRINGING ME THE PEACE OF MIND I WAS PROMISED.

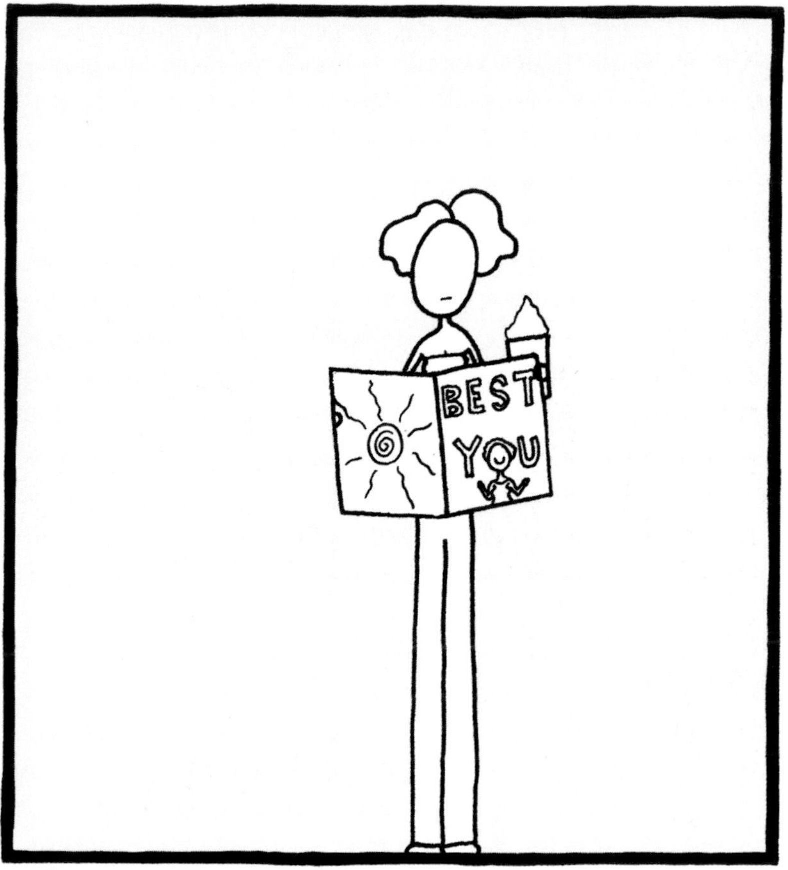
BEST
YOU

I DON'T MEAN TO BE INCONSIDERATE, BUT IF WE ALL REACH OUR HIGHEST CREATIVE POTENTIAL, WHO WILL SERVE ME MY EXTRA FOAMY CAFFÈ LATTE?

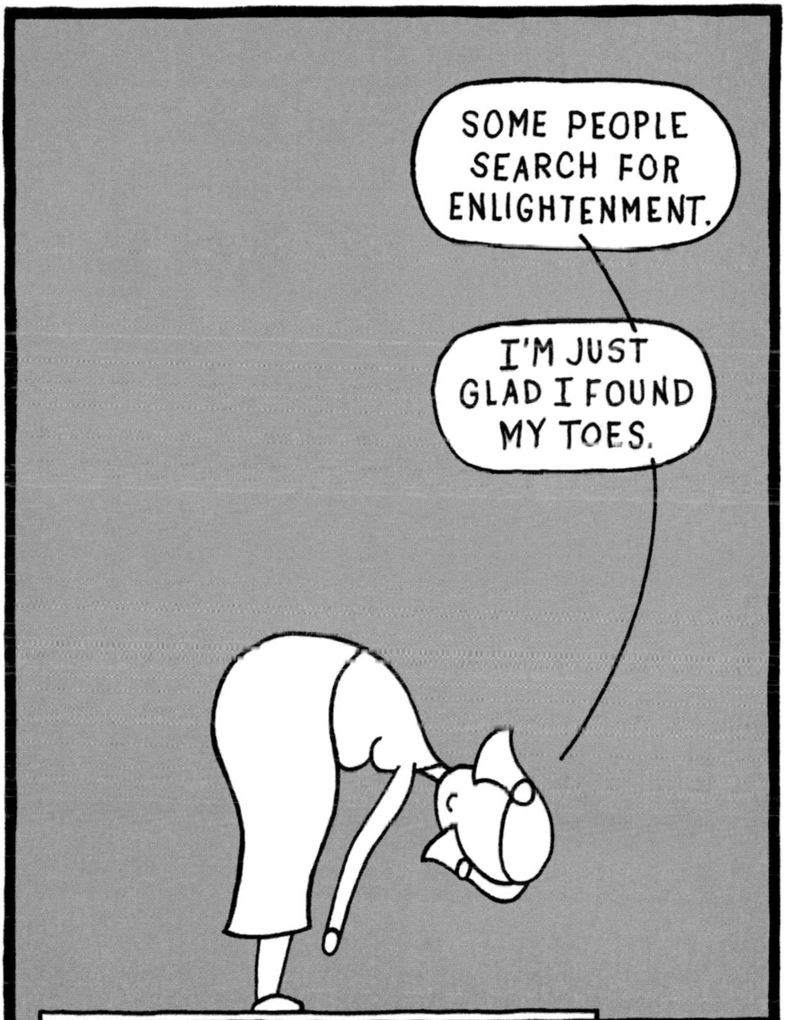
SOME PEOPLE SEARCH FOR ENLIGHTENMENT.
I'M JUST GLAD I FOUND MY TOES.

ACKNOWLEDGMENTS

Julia Jacques and the team at Adams Media, thank you for asking me if I'd be interested in making this book, as if I'd say anything but yes!

Joanna and Sandy, thank you for guiding me through the type of yoga practice I love. A strong, well-formed, slow practice that ends with a nice long rest, and leaves me centered and delighted to be alive.

Rina, thank you for being my best cartoonist friend, and for always taking time to give feedback on my first drafts.

Judy, thank you for saving me from grammatical embarrassment.

The Art Centre at Central Technical School, for guiding me while my style evolved, and for thickening my skin.

The women of BizNet, thank you for joining me in my entrepreneurial journey, and for allowing me to join you in yours.

Anna, thank you for being you, for letting me be me. For walks, laughs, tears, comfort, and more laughs. I could not ask for a better friend.

Joy, thank you for listening and providing a safe space for me to go deep and focus on what's most important.

Sylvia Catherine, for showing me what being non-judgmental looks like on this plane of existence. I hope you're enjoying the other side.

Anyu, thank you for always encouraging humor, and for saving every little thing I've produced since *Everyday People* cartoons were born.

Irving, thank you for always wishing the best for me. *Zay gezunt* to you as well.

Susan, thank you for being my number one supporter, craft show helper, listener of all my long-version tales of glory and woe, and for being the best little sister ever.

Fred, Evelyn, Leo, and Nina, thank you for welcoming me and always making room at your table for me to package my products.

Jessica, thank you for making it easy to be a work-at-home mom, and more recently for being my office assistant.

Tyler, thank you for drawing with me since you could hold a crayon, and for inspiring cartoon #638 (What do you want to be when you grow up? Myself.).

Terry, thank you for your never-ending support, and for letting me be me. I can't imagine a better person to share this life with, and I'm thankful that you feel the same way.

And thank you to every person who ever laughed at one of my cartoons. If you knew the extent to which I thought I was alone in my thoughts and feelings, you'd know just how much it means to me to know that you relate.

ABOUT THE AUTHOR

Cathy Thorne's *Everyday People* cartoons resonate with people who are doing the best they can in their never-ending quest for inner peace. Since its inception in 1999, this relatable, funny, and insightful cartoon has been featured in publications such as *The Toronto Star*, *The Sunday Telegraph*, *Good Housekeeping*, *Reader's Digest*, and *Huffington Post*. Cathy has been commissioned to create cartoons for Dove; BabyCenter; and Action on Addiction, which is supported by Catherine Middleton, Duchess of Cambridge.

When she's not writing and drawing cartoons, Cathy is filling her online shop with paper goods that remind everyday people to live mindfully or, when that seems too challenging, to have a good laugh.

Cathy lives and works on a quiet street in Toronto, Canada, with her husband and two children, who love her very much—and like her even more when she's living in the moment.